The World is Just a Book Away

The World is Just a Book Away

Edited by James J. Owens

WIJABA

USC Libraries

University of Southern California

Published by the USC Libraries Press
3550 Trousdale Parkway
University of Southern California
Los Angeles, CA 90089
libraries.usc.edu

ISBN: 978-0-9991348-0-1
Library of Congress Control Number: 2017952722

Miep Gies's essay, which originally appeared in *Anne Frank Remembered: The Story of the Woman Who Helped to Hide the Frank Family*, is reprinted here courtesy the author and the Estate of Miep Gies.

Sections of the essays by Naif al-Mutawa and the Dalai Lama have appeared in previously published works.

With respect for the original graphic mark of "The World is Just a Book Away," the editor has requested that the book consistently use a lowercase "is" when referring to the nonprofit or the publication.

Design by Silvina Niepomniszcze
Illustrations by Ryane Acalin
Edited by James J. Owens
Printed and bound by Ace Commercial, Santa Fe Springs

To my mother Virginia Heydenreich Owens,
who read to me, and to my son Alexander,
to whom I read.

CONTENTS

ACKNOWLEDGMENTS

The World is Just a Book Away was fifteen years in the making. I am deeply grateful to each of the sixty participants for sharing their personal stories about books and reading. Extensive networking and the collective efforts of hundreds of people were required to create this book. It would be impossible for me to state the role that each individual played. Thus, like the book, these acknowledgments are alphabetized with my heartfelt gratitude.

Anne Hamilton Abouchar, Craig Abouchar, Doug Abrams, Luis Placido de Abreu, Ryane Acalin, Amy Achron, Josette Aggarwal, Punit Aggarwal, Jaffar Agha, Sara Agha, Gitti Akbari, Mindy Alberman, Zaia Alexander, David López Álvarez, Doug Andrews, Helen Gill Arnold, Dhian Astrita, Aziz, Chris Bard, Gabriela Serna Barrera, Alexandra Diez Barroso, Daniela Diez Barroso, Emilio Diez Barroso, Michal Beaumont, Lauren S. Beck, Pippa Beng, Steven Bennett, Liz Bernstein, John Bertrand, Chuck Binder, Jeff Bishop, Abby Blossom, Chris Boehm, Leslie Bogart, Martin Bongard, Drew Boyles, James Breech, Rebecca Bregman, Lavinia Browne, Melissa Buckman, Bryant Budiman, Natasha Budiman, Billy Buffington, Michelle Burke, Colleen Camp, Don Camp, Kate Campaigne, Joana Cannon, Lisa Cannon, Allison Caragan, Nicole C. Carey, Teresita Casipe-Bellon, Celeste Castro, Cécile Chahid-Nouraï, Baldwin H. Chambless, Emma Chapman, Roselle Kline Chartock, Barbara Chisholm, Kevin Chiu, Nangsa Chodon, Sharon Choe, Chupah, Maura Chwastky, Michael N. Cohen, Matt Coleman, Amanda Collins, Reeve Collins, Jamie Contompasis, Pauline Coughlan, Rudolph F. Crew, Carlos Antonio Crooks, Christine Owens-Crawford, Claudia Cross, Anne Maureen D'Ambrosio, Lee Ann Daly, Patricia Damon, Lori A. Dando, Frank D'Andrea, J Taylor D'Andrea, Arif Darmawan, Marissa DeCuir, Nanci Del Pico, Ruth DeSarno, Carmen Díaz, Nancy Ellen Dodd, Victoria Domínguez de Alcahúd, Teresa Doolan, Beth Dowd, Darby Drake, Denis Draper, Benoit Dupuis, AnneMarie Durcan, Alice Dutton, Mark Edlitz, Joshua H. Eichenstein, James G. Ellis, Averill Emery, Josiah Emery, Shirin Ershadi, Hillery Estes, Phillip Evans, David Fahey, Francesca L. Fartaj, Maxamillian Feldman, Shawn Ferguson, Laura Ferretti, Susan Fink, Maeve Fiona, Michael Fisk, Noël Riley Fitch, Vivian Ford, Cassandra Pataky Fowler, Catherine Fox, Marjorie François, Lisa Frechette, Brian Fried, Hugh Garvey, Tyson Gaskill, Zsa Zsa Gershick, Bryan Gibbs, David Gies, Erwin Gies, Jeanine Gies, Paul Gies, Betsy Gill, Colleen Gillmore, Alexis Giusfred, David Goddard, Jana Godshall, Heather Goldman, Jane Goodall, Atsal Gormley, Gita Govahi, Alan Green, Joe Grogan,

Veronica Grogan, Max Gross, Diego Gutierrez, Patricia Gvozdich, Beth Hallmark, S. J. Harker, George Hegarty, Dale Henry, Alexa Herron, James G. Heydenreich, Sam Hiersteiner, Scott Hitomi, Julienne Ho, Nancy Hobson, AnneMarie Holian, JoAnn Holm, Ben Hopkins, Jessie Hopkins, Nina Houghton, Cathryn Hu, Mary R. Hulnick, H. Ronald Hulnick, Laura Hume, Adam Hutchison, Ben Jackson, Lauren Janes, Atrayah Janhe, Abhinay Jhaveri, A. G. S. Johnson, Holly Johnson, Robin Jonas, Gede Karnada, Marilyn Kaye, Victoria Kennedy, Angela Kent, Dana B. Kershner, David W. Kershner, Riz Khan, Tahir S. Khan, Kristina Kiehl, Nathan Kilcer, Bob Kilroy, Alex Kim, John J. Kirkpatrick, Stuart Kirkpatrick, Christina Korp, Tom Kozicki, Joeri Kreisberg, Paulinka Kreisberg, Patty LaMagna, Brooke Lange, Peter Launsky-Tieffenthal, Autumn Lennon, Laura Clark Leon, Sharon Lester, Oded Levy, Mary Lewis, Vanessa Hendriadi Li, Michelle Lincoln, Jacki Lippman, Diane Bloom Litvak, David Livingston, Meaghan Lloyd, Rishabh Singh Loomba, Trilok Singh Loomba, Tom K. Lopach, Victoria Lucai, Shannon Max MacMillan, Cybella Maffitt, Ciara Mahon, Mehmet Mahruki, Marti Maniatas, Tina Manning, Clare H. Manz, Kimberley Marchant, Claire Dupuis le Marois, Pam Martinson, Debbie Masterson, Tamu Matose, Jessy May, Shirley Maxey, Ainsley McCaa, Stephanie Platt McCaa, Meg McCarthy, Hugh Thomas McHarg, Christine McManus, Adrienne Medawar, Trudi Mergili, Lisa Merkele, Annette Ponnock Meyers, Adam Miller, Brent Miller, Melody Miller, Jenny Ming, Sarah Minneman, Jessica Minton, Zainab Mirza, Lorna Mitchell, Kiyomi D. Mizukami, Moilé-Moilé, Jaron Moler, Tim Monich, Andy Morrow, Will Morrow, Lamiya Morshed, Eric Mullen, Dawn Mumm, Suzanne Munson, Rae Lynn Murillo, Bernadette A. Musgrave, Stephan Muzzonigro, Susana B. Name, Liam Neeson, Dirk Nevelle, Silvina Niepomniszcze, Alyssa Nobriga, Jenny Nuber, Judith Olah, Gina Olaya, Paige Smith Orloff, Sabbir Ahmed Osmani, Alexander James Owens, Charlotte A. Owens, Gail Owens, John Owens, Mary Anne McManus Owens, Virgina Heydenreich Owens, Mia Pak, Pavel Palazhchenko, Mary Paris, Chuck Pembroke, Ann Pendley, Marilyn Pessin, Jacob Petersen, Mia Petrarca, Damian Pherigo, Marion Philadelphia, Andrew Pietra, Travis Pinkner, Francis Poon, Elizabeth Querbes, Catherine Quinlan, Juan Manuel Quiroga, Christina Rasch, Alexis Rasten, Lorna Y. Reed, Marco Antonio Regil, Licia Rester-Frazee, Rizo, Christine Rodsater, Shani Rosenzweig, Ingrid Rowland, Jennifer Ruiz, Kelly Safrit, Gayle Samek, Cecilia Santiago-Gonzalez, Farah Mustika Sari, Aram Saroyan, Jacqui Schock, Julie Schoerke, Michael Schwartz, Reed Semcken, Kathryn Sermak, Betty Sheinbaum, Stanley K. Sheinbaum, Tenzin Sherab, Arundhati Dé Sheth, Sahil Sheth, Anthony Shriver, Bobby Shriver, Maria Shriver, Mark Shriver, Timothy Shriver, Claire Shropshire, Marcela Sofia

Silva, Dina Silver, Ann Simpson, Joe Sive, Heather Smith, Ashley Parker Snider, Charlie Soap, Alexander Souri, Ashley Stahl, Craig Stanford, Michael Starratt, Andru Subowo, Cornelis Suijk, Eric Sullano, Sue Symth, Syahrizal Taher, Tenzin Taklha, J. Todd Thaxton, Robert Thurman, Emma Tillinger, Chiara Towne, Penpa Tsering, Jessica Tuck, Debra Tucker, Mpho Tutu, Kim Twing, Debbie Vandermeulen, Rob Varnas, Cindy C. Villa, Jacobi Wade, Jesse Walker, Adlai Wertman, Evelyne Bronwyn Werzowa, Stephanie Wetzel, Jenny Wharton, Gregory G. White, Wendy White, Sara Wigal, Sarinda Parsons Wilson, Russell Wiser, Michelle Valenzuela Wolf, Jared Wolfson, Nomi Yah, Jason Yanagihara, Amelia Young, Deena Yunus, Monica Yunus, Arie Victoria Yusuf, Camille Zamora, Danny Zappin, Greg Zappin

PREFACE BY CATHERINE QUINLAN

The pleasure of *The World is Just a Book Away* is the pleasure of discovering the words that motivate scientists, inspire artists, and shape the worldviews of senators, presidents, and prime ministers. Everyone who reads the essays James Owens has collected here will find much to admire, many perspectives to consider and with which to agree or disagree, and new paths to explore the previously unknown. *The World is Just a Book Away* is a lively and delightful embodiment of why words, stories, books, and libraries matter so immensely to humans and to humanity.

On the day of my official installation as dean of the University of Southern California Libraries, I told a story of my own—the story of sitting on my mother's lap as a child, looking at the letters and spaces on pages of books as she read aloud. I remember the feeling, the very particular sort of joy, when I realized that those marks on the page carried meaning, that they *were* the stories my mother was telling me.

I have worked for many years, as a librarian and a library leader, to make such joy possible for as many people as I can and to inspire in others the drive to seek out the rewards of intellectual discovery. And discovery does not happen spontaneously or of its own accord. It requires work. The particular kind of work, at its most foundational, is learning to read and write.

I paused, writing that last sentence, stopping myself before I wrote, "*simply* learning to read and write." Understanding and being able to use the written word is so essential to our intellectual, cultural, and social lives that it is far too easy to take for granted. But learning, and making learning possible and likely, is neither simple nor easy.

The global average for adult literacy is 86%; 750 million people cannot read or write.[1] A complex web of political, economic, and cultural factors influences literacy rates. One of those factors is particularly relevant to those of us involved with the World is Just a Book Away (WIJABA) nonprofit and its work building libraries—the availability and accessibility of books.

A 2012 study of fourth-grade students in forty countries found that the health of a library in a school or community was the strongest predictor of reading proficiency among the factors the scholars reviewed—as the report put it, "But what is clear is that libraries definitely matter, and they matter a lot."[2]

Books in well-equipped schools, public libraries that support their communities, books available to curious and eager children when and where they need them—all of that has the potential to improve literacy. By creating libraries in places of need, WIJABA is working toward that potential on a worldwide scale.

The statistics inform, perhaps make us angry, but the stories inspire. That is the critical purpose of this book—capturing stories of the enchantment of reading and sharing them as broadly as possible. I was delighted to learn about Yo-Yo Ma's thoughts on *The Little Prince*, Ambassador Jeane Kirkpatrick's love of *Nancy Drew* and *Madame Bovary*, and Archbishop Tutu's fascination with a Marvel Comics character. Consider what the world would have lost had such accomplished people not had those words, sentences, and stories to inspire them.

This book has sixty such stories, and I am grateful to James for bringing them together and for inviting me and the USC Libraries to join him in bringing them to the world. With James's leadership, the World is Just a Book Away organization has built ninety libraries and made thousands upon thousands of books available to school-age children in Indonesia, Mexico, and the United States. WIJABA has accomplished much, yet in many ways is just beginning to make an incredible difference.

As a WIJABA advisory board member, as a dean of a university library, and as a human being with a profound respect for learning and the advancement of knowledge, I am delighted that the profits from this book will help build more libraries, buy even more books, and make possible the joy of discovery for as-yet-untold numbers of people. It is indeed the world that will benefit from the passion, dedication, and persistence that James and all who work with him lend to this most worthy of humanitarian causes.

September 8th, 2017

[1] UNESCO Institute for Statistics, "Literacy Rates Continue to Rise from One Generation to the Next," UIS Fact Sheet, no. 45 (September 2017), 3.

[2] Stephen Krashen, Syying Lee, and Jeff McQuillan, "Is the Library Important? Multivariate Studies at the National and International Level," *Journal of Language and Literacy Education*, vol. 8, no. 1 (2012), 26–38.

FOREWORD BY JANE GOODALL

During a single year I meet thousands of people. And of these thousands there are only a very few that lead to meaningful, ongoing relationships. I first met James Owens, the editor of this fascinating book—*The World is Just a Book Away*—in 2003. It was then that he asked if I would agree to participate in this book. And I agreed, because books have always played a really important part in my life.

When I was a child my mother read me a story each night, and from the start it was stories about animals that I most wanted to hear. *Peter Rabbit* and the other Beatrix Potter books were favorites. We had very little money when I was growing up. World War II broke out, and my mother, sister, and I went to live with my grandmother in Bournemouth in the Birches, a Victorian red brick house that is now the family home. We couldn't afford new books (and not many were printed in the war) so most of my books came from the local library. My mother, realizing I would learn to read more quickly if the books were about what I loved best, selected those about animals. Some of my favorites were Kipling's *The Jungle Book* and *The Just So Stories*. And Kenneth Grahame's *The Wind in the Willows*. Then, when I was eight years old, I fell in love with Hugh Lofting's *The Story of Doctor Doolittle*—I reread it under the bedclothes, with a flashlight, the night before it had to go back to the library. And that Christmas my grandmother gave me one of the best presents I had ever had— my very own copy of that book.

When I was ten years old I discovered a small second-hand bookshop and used to spend hours there. One day I found a copy of *Tarzan of the Apes*. I had just enough money, saved up from the few pennies pocket money I got each week, to buy it. I took it up into the branches of my favorite tree, Beech (which is still there in the garden, though too tall now for me to climb!) And of course, I fell in love with the glorious lord of the jungle—and was really jealous when he married the wrong Jane! I still have that book, as well as the precious *Doctor Doolittle* book, in my bedroom in the Birches—along with all the other hundreds of books I have acquired over the years.

It was reading about Doctor Doolittle and Mowgli that crystalized my fascination for animals of all sorts. And it was because of the Tarzan books that I decided I would grow up, go to Africa, live with wild animals—and write books about them. Thinking that she would give me a great treat, my mother saved up to take me to the local cinema to see a Johnny Weissmuller *Tarzan* film. After a few moments I began to cry, and had to be taken out by my shocked mother. "But that wasn't Tarzan" I sobbed. It was my own imagined Tarzan with whom I had fallen in love, not someone pretending to be Tarzan.

That story highlights how important books can be in developing a child's imagination. In this era of TV and virtual reality it is more important than ever to ensure that children have access to books—which is one reason I have written so many books for children.

If it was books that helped shape my dreams, it was my mother whose wisdom enabled me to achieve those dreams. When I first talked about my desire to go and live with animals in Africa everyone laughed at me—girls did not do that sort of thing in the 1940s. But my mother would simply say that I would have to "work hard, take advantage of opportunities, and never give up." I have shared those words with children around the world through my talks and books and it is wonderful how many young people have told me, "You taught me that because you did it, I can do it too."

Although James did not know my mother's words when he began this project more than fifteen years ago, I have come to realize, as I have got to know him better, that he certainly lives by this principal. It was a herculean task that he set himself, to compile and edit this book, and it could not have been achieved without hard work, seizing opportunities as they arose—and never giving up.

And how wonderful that the creation of this book has led to the creation also of a fantastic organization—The World is Just a Book Away (WIJABA). This charity promotes literacy to thousands of children through its libraries and programs. And, most recently, this has led to an exciting collaboration between WIJABA and the Jane Goodall Institute's environmental and humanitarian education program for young people of all ages, Jane Goodall's Roots & Shoots, now in one hundred countries.

Roots & Shoots was created because I was meeting students everywhere who seemed to have little hope for the future. They were mostly apathetic, but some were depressed, some were angry. "You have compromised our future," they told me. "And there is nothing we can do about it."

Indeed, we have compromised our children's future. In my lifetime, the population on our planet has more than tripled and this is increasingly putting a strain on the finite natural resources of our small planet Earth. We are destroying habitats, polluting air, water, and land, causing climate change. More and more plants and animals are becoming gravely endangered, and many are already extinct. But I do not agree with those who say there is nothing we can do about it. I believe there is still hope, but only if we get together to counteract unsustainable Western lifestyles, and the crippling poverty that causes people to destroy the environment as they try to make a living. The most important message of Roots & Shoots is that each one of us matters, each one of us has a role to play, each one of us makes a difference every day. And we can choose what sort of difference we make. Roots & Shoots is about working on projects that make the world a better place for people, animals, and the environment we all share.

At age eighty-two, I am still on the road some three hundred days per year. It is a crazy schedule but I believe it is my mission not only to raise awareness about the harm we are doing to the environment, but also to spread the message of hope. And my greatest hope for the future lies in the energy and commitment of children once they understand the problems facing us and are empowered to take action. This is why I am so excited by the collaboration between Roots & Shoots and WIJABA.

In July 2014, I had the honor of opening a WIJABA library in Bali, Indonesia, which was named in my honor. Afterward I wrote to James, "WIJABA libraries are very obviously making a huge difference to hundreds of children. Just watching the way the children pick up the books and read them, and the expression in their eyes and their excitement, makes everything worthwhile." That day James had a fabulous surprise for me. In honor of my eightieth birthday, WIJABA had committed to launching The World is Just a Book Away Environmental Education Program at eighty schools—in partnership with Jane Goodall's Roots & Shoots! I could not have possibly asked for—or dreamed of—a better birthday present.

Partnership has been an essential component in expanding Jane Goodall's Roots & Shoots chapters to hundreds of thousands of children around the world. It is as a result of the continued partnership with WIJABA that more than 250 schools in Indonesia will soon have access to a five-week educational program culminating in the establishment of a Roots & Shoots chapter. Some six thousand children will then be deciding how they can best affect change in their own environment, rolling up their sleeves, and taking action.

And in 2015, we announced the expansion of this partnership to the children served by WIJABA in Mexico. Who knows where this will end. Back in 2003, when I completed my essay for this book, I had no idea how much the project would grow, that it would turn into a children's literacy charity, that WIJABA libraries would be named in my honor, or that this wonderful partnership to expand Roots & Shoots would unfold. Surely James and I met for a reason.

In reading *The World is Just a Book Away*, people may at first wonder what James and I have in common with this eclectic group of people ranging from Queen Noor and Vanessa Redgrave, to Yo-Yo Ma and Edward M. Kennedy, to Martin Scorsese, Liam Neeson, Muhammad Yunus, the Dalai Lama, and many more. The answer is a passion for books and reading.

The World is Just a Book Away is a unique record, a treasury, of how and why a diverse set of people, including many who have made enormous political, ethical, scientific, and creative choices, have been influenced by reading books. These are their stories. Each one is a window into how books and reading have helped to shape the lives of the people in this book.

Anyone who reads *The World is Just a Book Away* will find something moving, something intriguing, something inspirational. They will discover books they never thought of, and many will dream ideas, large and small, that will change our world.

Jane Goodall

January 12th, 2017

INTRODUCTION BY JAMES J. OWENS

Books have always been my refuge. I cannot imagine my life without them. In fact one book, *The Encyclopedia of World Travel*, is at the center of my earliest memory.

I am sitting on my mother's lap in the living room of our small apartment on Castle Hill Avenue in Great Barrington, Massachusetts. I can see books all around me—ordered neatly on shelves and even lined up along a board on top of the old-fashioned, cast-iron radiator behind me. The chair is green. It has a deep weave. I love sitting in it with my mother as she reads, tracing my fingers over and around the pattern, imagining rivers, and mountains, and oceans, and far off lands.

"What is that?" I say, pointing at the cover. "Those are the pyramids of Giza, Jimmy, built by the great pharaohs of ancient Egypt." I gaze at the man in flowing robes sitting on top of a camel in front of the huge stone monuments. "Is it far away?" I ask. "Very far away, in the North of Africa," she replies. "Can we go there someday?" I ask. And my mother, who always taught me that I could do anything I wanted says, "Yes, Jimmy, one day we will go to Egypt, and climb the pyramid, and ride a camel."

Is this an actual memory? A memory of a memory? A memory pieced together from fragments of childhood images? Or, is it an idealized scene I created in my active imagination?

I cannot say for sure. Memory is a tricky thing. I can say that this feels like a memory. I can also say that *The Encyclopedia of World Travel*—which sits beside me as I write this introduction—had a deep impact on my dreams and my path in life.

Other books were part of my daily routine. We visited the children's section of Mason Library every two weeks and borrowed the maximum number of books. Each night, my mother read to my sister Christine and me from those books and our own children's books stacked on the small shelf in our room: *The Aristocats, Georgie Mouse Finds a House, Lady and the Tramp, Soda Pop, The Busy Bulldozer, Choo Choo—The Little Switch Engine*, and my particular favorite, *The Wreck that Was Hesperas*, about an old car that finds a new home. Reading to us always made my mother smile—her voice slowing with mystery or squeaking with excitement.

I remember the feeling of being read to. It made me feel safe. It made me feel loved.

———

When I was about nine, my mother's world started to unravel. She spent more and more time in bed. She no longer laughed and smiled. She seemed to be slipping away.

It was 1974, before people understood depression, or how to deal with it, and before the advent of effective antidepressants. In desperation, my mother checked herself into a psychiatric hospital, thinking it would make her better. It only made her worse. People convinced her that she would end up in a state institution, which terrified her. She lost hope.

Each visit to the hospital was more painful than the last. I wanted my mother back. My mother who read and sang, and danced around the kitchen. My mother who baked us special birthday cakes shaped like a fish, a rocking horse, and a butterfly. My mother who believed in me and dreamed with me.

I could see the great effort it took for her to smile when it came time for us to leave. I felt like I was abandoning her. I wanted to rescue her. I couldn't.

"I'll never understand what happened to me," she wrote in her last letter to her own mother, which I received many years later. "My children . . . are so beautiful and deserved so much more."

During that seemingly endless summer when we went to live with my father's mother, I escaped from my pain and my fear into the pages of books.

———

After several months in the hospital, my mother received a weekend break late in August. She seemed sadder, more tired. She asked me to always keep her picture, so I wouldn't forget what she looked like. I was terrified, but I didn't know what to do.

I remember every detail of her last morning.

My sister and I are sitting on the living room floor playing cards. We jump up when our mother comes over. She hugs and kisses us. She tells us she loves us. She says she is going upstairs to take a nap. I watch her climb the stairs.

Several hours later, my grandmother sends me to get her for lunch. Instinctively, I know something is wrong. My body tenses as I grip the banister, as I stare down at the turquoise carpet, as I turn the cold glass doorknob.

My memory shatters.

My father's van skidding to a halt. Sirens. People racing up the stairs. Seeing the black car. Knowing what the black car means.

No one talked about trauma or counseling. "Say your mother died of natural causes," we were told. But I saw the looks. I heard the whispers. I felt the shame.

At seventy-one, my grandmother took care of us. Because her house only had three bedrooms, I shared a room with my father—the room with the cold glass doorknob. Everything I had known—my toys, the furniture, my mother's belongings—everything except my clothes and some books—was boxed up. Stored away. Gone. Just like my mother.

⸻

I only have very fragmented memories from the next four or five years. I didn't feel safe. I didn't fit in. So, I shut the world out. However, my memory clears again in middle school when I began to have more friends. But, books were still my main refuge. I was addicted to Charles Dickens and, to a lesser degree, Mark Twain. *Gone with the Wind* took me a whole month and sparked my interest in the Civil War. *Les Misérables* was next, igniting my lifelong passion for French history.

When I was in high school my father remarried. Charlotte was a stabilizing force. I finally had a room of my own—a small sanctuary filled with my own books and books belonging to three generations of my mother's family.

School became a source of pleasure, exploration, and success. In Dr. Roselle Chartock's history class we read the anthology she coedited—*The Holocaust Years: Society on Trial*, which inspired me to read everything I could find about World War II and reinforced my desire to one day write a book. In Mr. Field's class we created a lifeline—mine stretched on for an optimistic 125 years. I recently rediscovered it and was amazed by how much had come to fruition: learning French and German, university degrees, traveling the world.

Most surprisingly, I'd written that I would help to build schools for children in developing countries.

However, during my senior year, I suffered my first bout of depression, and finally understood the desperation my mother had felt. But, I had access to therapy and resources that weren't readily available to her in the 1970s. And, as I have always done, I sought comfort in books, losing myself in the complex plots of great Russian novels like *War and Peace, Anna Karenina, Crime and Punishment,* and *The Brothers Karamazov*.

⸻

Bates College opened a whole new world for me. I studied French and history, immersed myself in French authors and playwrights—Balzac, Dumas, Ionesco, Molière, Proust—and worked at Ladd Library. Then, during my junior year, the adventures I'd dreamed and read about for so long started to become reality. I moved to Europe, studied in Nice, France, and traveled to fourteen countries.

After college, my world further expanded when I lived in Paris, London, and Munich working for Louis Vuitton, Coca-Cola, and Agfa-Gavaert. Although these were wonderful career opportunities, I still didn't feel like I fit in.

During my frequent trips to Africa for Coca-Cola, I visited some of the poorest areas of Kenya, Senegal, the Republic of the Congo, Cameroon, and Gabon. From days spent in streets of mud, endless rows of shacks, and open sewage drains, I would return to the air-conditioned luxury of my hotel at night to read. Invariably, my mind drifted back to the people I'd met—particularly the children—who clearly deserved so much more than what life had dealt them.

I had an enduring feeling that I was called upon to do something else, to use the privileges afforded to me by my career and education to accomplish something different—but I didn't know what.

After leaving my job in Munich and before matriculating at Columbia University for my MBA, I traveled to Egypt, fulfilling the pact I had made with my mother so many years before.

Early one morning in Cairo, when it was still dark outside, I hired a driver to take me to Giza. I am not sure that it was permitted then or now, but a security guard allowed me to climb the "small pyramid," built by Menkaure, which is *only* approximately twenty stories tall. Given my fear of heights and stones that were more like giant blocks I had to clamber over than steps—this was no small feat.

The sky was still gray when I made it to the top and pointed my hands above my head, completing the shape of the pyramid. Tears streamed down my face as I looked out over the great Sahara and said, "We made it."

At that moment a lone Bedouin in flowing robes rode his camel to the base of Menkaure's pyramid and stared up at me. He patiently waited for me to descend, before offering me a ride on his camel. The cover of *The Encyclopedia of World Travel* had come to life.

It took my breath away.

Since that moment in Egypt, I have never doubted the power of words and imagery.

My lifelong relationship with books sprouted into what seemed like a simple idea in 2002 when I decided to create *The World is Just a Book Away*, an anthology about how books and reading influenced the lives of prominent people. However, creating this book turned out to be anything but simple. Many prominent people receive hundreds or even thousands of requests to participate in worthwhile projects every year.

By 2008, the book had gained momentum and I realized that if I could launch a charity to promote children's literacy, donate my profit from the book to the organization, and tap into the collective energy of people affiliated with the book, something even greater than the book itself was within reach.

The World is Just a Book Away (WIJABA), the charity, was born in October of 2008. From the beginning, my faith that I had made the right choice was reinforced as people came forward to help. Each board member, advisory board member, ambassador, and volunteer played a vital role, as have the hundreds of donors throughout the years.

We began our work in Sidoarjo, Indonesia—a region devastated by the world's worst mudflow disaster, which engulfed sixteen villages and displaced more than thirty thousand people. The schools I visited on my first trip were overcrowded and in various states of disrepair. None had a library. None of the children had access to the types of books many of us take for granted.

After careful consideration, we decided to build libraries at primary schools or orphanages in hubs of approximately twenty-five to develop long-term community relationships, meaningfully include local staff, and eventually shepherd the libraries into learning centers for programs.

Although we focused on sustainability over growth, WIJABA grew faster than I'd anticipated. We expanded into Padang, Sumatra, after the earthquake and tsunami and then to Bali after learning about the thousands of children living in orphanages on that beautiful island. In 2012, we launched our first library for the children of Chihuahua, Mexico, who were at high risk due to gang violence sparked by the drug trade. And, most recently, after learning about charter schools in Los Angeles that had no libraries, we decided to create a pilot project closer to home.

Nine years after its launch, WIJABA has ninety libraries and two mobile libraries that have served more than seventy thousand children in three countries (Indonesia, Mexico, and the United States). We have also created an environmental education program in partnership with Jane Goodall's Roots & Shoots, which is being introduced at more than 250 schools in Indonesia and Mexico.

It seems like nothing short of a miracle.

Before WIJABA, the different chapters of my circuitous life always felt like a disjointed story that I couldn't assemble into a cohesive tale. However, since our launch, that multifaceted picture has come increasingly into focus.

The sense of purpose I gained through teaching, writing, and working on the book, was reinforced by the birth of my son Alexander in 2005. With him, I have the blessing of experiencing the miracle of childhood through the endless wonder

The Mason's
Soup & Salad Dinner

Friday
April 12
6:00 pm

Masonic Hall
428 N. Main Street
in Fort Bragg

$15 ticket
Library
Benefit

Come help **Friends of the Fort Bragg Library** raise funds for library expansion by attending a Soup & Salad Dinner at Masonic Hall.

Doors open at 6. Dinner at 7.

Along with a smorgasbord of delicious soups there will be salad, French bread and a dessert. The price is $15 per person with all proceeds benefiting the **Fort Bragg Library Expansion Project.**

Door Prize!
Great Food!

Questions? Call Library at 964-2020.

of my own child. His world, of course, always included books, from the waterproof ones he chewed on in the bathtub, to my own childhood books that migrated with me to Santa Monica, to the series he devours about knights, dragons, and magical creatures.

As I write this, Alexander is twelve and we still read together. *Harry Potter and the Prisoner of Azkaban* is our latest. He says, "Books spark your imagination. Reading even one page can change your life."

I feel that, in reading to my own son, and in sharing my love of books with thousands of children across the world, I am continuing the legacy my mother imparted to me—one of exploration, passion, possibility and—most importantly—hope.

Each time I have the privilege of opening a new WIJABA library, I shake hands or high-five every child present—even when there are four or five hundred children at a school. Many of these children have never met a foreigner and the library opening represents a new beginning—a ray of hope in lives that have all too often been shrouded in darkness.

I know that many of these children live in heart-wrenching circumstances. Many of their schools are derelict. Some of them have no safe place to do their homework. I know that WIJABA won't change the lives of all these children. However, for many of them, WIJABA's books, libraries, and educational programs will fuel dreams of becoming doctors and nurses; engineers and architects; firefighters and teachers; farmers and scientists. Even presidents.

When I read to the children in our libraries, we often dissolve into laughter because I can't speak Indonesian or Spanish and mispronounce words. This is always a special moment for me. In our shared laughter and in our shared love of books, I can see the light in their eyes. I can see the hope on their faces. I can see the world expanding before them.

───────

By 2015, the charity had more help, the pressure on my own schedule had eased, and I felt that I could concentrate on the book once again. That same year Catherine Quinlan, dean of the University of Southern California Libraries learned about *The World is Just a Book Away* and expressed an immediate interest in publishing it through USC Libraries Press. USC has been my academic home for more than twenty years and the Trojan Family has been instrumental in developing both the book and the charity.

Thus, my book about the books that inspired prominent people is being published by a library press to help buy books and build libraries for children who have none.

It feels like a perfect circle in my life and in my relationship with reading and books.

At times it seemed impossible to finish *The World is Just a Book Away*. At times it took me more than four years and thirty or more points of contact to finalize a single participant. During the fifteen years that this book has been part of my life, I couldn't count the number of times I felt like giving up.

But, I didn't give up. Creating *The World is Just a Book Away* strengthened my belief that—with an authentic vision, hard work, and perseverance—things will happen when they are supposed to happen. If, for example, I had published the book early in the process, I might never have realized my greater purpose of launching the charity and promoting children's literacy.

As I close this introduction, many of my childhood dreams have come true. I am a father, a professor, a writer, and a traveler. However, no childhood dream could have prepared me for the miracles that have unfolded through this book and through founding WIJABA. Over the years, I have learned that all experiences— even the most tragic—hold within them the possibility of creating something that can bring light into the world and ultimately inspire us to be of service.

Yet, the little boy, Jimmy Owens from Great Barrington, Massachusetts, still resides within me. It is he who inspires me to touch the lives of children who feel alone, afraid, and unheard. If just one child feels seen, finds solace, discovers hope, or pursues a dream through books purchased from the proceeds of *The World is Just a Book Away*, my mission will be fulfilled.

It is also the younger version of myself—the dreamer, the reader, the child who believed anything was possible—who helps to drive me forward. I feel honored and humbled that the sixty people in this book who have inspired the world in so many different ways have entrusted me with their stories.

My heartfelt aspiration is that *The World is Just a Book Away* will inspire you to explore books you might never have considered, embarking upon journeys into new worlds and magical realms of knowledge, imagination, endless possibilities, and hope.

June 12th, 2017

BUZZ ALDRIN

"Throughout the years, I have been marked by the words
and books of many great authors."

"Magnificent desolation." These two words were the first I uttered when I set foot on the moon on July 20th, 1969. They are very powerful and emotional words that described my spontaneous feelings as I stepped off Apollo 11 as part of the first manned mission to the moon, knowing that we were farther from earth than anyone had ever been before us.

I find that words are magical in their ability to capture emotion and convey information. Perhaps that is why I have always been intrigued by the spoken word and the written word.

Throughout the years, I have been marked by the words and books of many great authors. I particularly enjoy historical fiction; and *The Winds of War* and *War and Remembrance* by Herman Wouk stand out as having left a lasting impression on me. Through the lives of Naval Captain Victor "Pug" Henry and his family, these books chronicle the period leading up to, during, and immediately following World War II.

Rather than teaching or relating details of this turbulent time through dry facts, Wouk brings the period to life. Through his narrative, vivid descriptions, historical details, and complex characters, he succeeds in transporting his readers back through time.

As people who lived through the World War II age die off, I think it's extremely important that future generations continue to learn about this period in time. Books such as Wouk's, *The Winds of War* and *War and Remembrance* help future generations understand the importance of this era. In doing so, these books also help readers understand that, without the struggles and sacrifices of the brave people who lived in that time, our world would be a very different place.

Buzz Aldrin

October 23rd, 2005

HER MAJESTY QUEEN NOOR
AL HUSSEIN OF JORDAN

"I have observed on countless occasions how hope and a sense of purpose propagate even in the harshest climate of war, poverty, catastrophe, and prejudice."

As someone with roots in both East and West, who has spent most of a lifetime trying to build bridges between Arab and American cultures, I, like so many others from around the world, have struggled to make sense of the events during and since September 11th, 2001. In a world where people experience increasing levels of fear and insecurity and bear witness to untold atrocities, there exists another equally troubling reality: the growth of a dangerous social, economic, and cultural divide between East and West and a deep lack of understanding in the West and even within the Muslim world about the true principles and values of Islam—a faith that once spread social, cultural, scientific, and political enlightenment throughout the world and today is practiced by 1.2 billion people.

In my quest to promote genuine global peace and security, and build bridges of cultural understanding, one book has provided me with a much-needed insightful examination of the universal values and aspirations that all people share, regardless of race, religion, creed, or gender. Imam Feisal Abdul Rauf's book entitled *What's Right with Islam* offers an illuminating and hopeful voice about not only what is right with Islam, but also what is right with America.

Imam Feisal's words and vision point the way toward a revived enlightenment throughout the world where voices of reason, compassion, and moderation in all religions will drown out those preaching intolerance, hate, and division; where passionate moderates among Muslims, Christians, and Jews will embrace the common values shared by the three Abrahamic faiths—the respect for freedom, justice, and compassion summed up in the commandment of our one God to love others as we love ourselves.

It is my sincere hope that we will hear more of the Muslim voices around the world, such as Imam Feisal Abdul Rauf, who are inspiring a more balanced, thoughtful, and open public discourse on the stereotypes of harem, hijab, and holy war that so dominate Western media and public perceptions of Islam today. They are beginning to challenge the extremist, misogynistic paradigm that distorts the true roots of Islam. Their conviction helps unlock the patriarchal traditions that have distorted Islam's message of equality, liberty, and justice for all.

What's Right with Islam addresses the difficult fears, stereotypes, and realities that exist in our modern world and demonstrates that no one culture or nation has the monopoly on virtue or intolerance. Such qualities are not apportioned geographically or by religion. Yet, this book shows that faith, one of the most compelling wellsprings of human action, can "contribute to an understanding and construction of a global notion of the common good."

Imam Feisal tackles our "ever-present challenge to bridge the gap between ideals and realities" and offers concrete steps by which people of all faith traditions can live together in peace. His description of a renewed vision of what "the good society" can be builds on the best roots of the American democratic system with the shared ethical underpinnings within Islam, Christianity, and Judaism.

I have observed on countless occasions how hope and a sense of purpose propagate even in the harshest climate of war, poverty, catastrophe, and prejudice. No matter how dire the circumstances, there are always individuals looking to a better tomorrow, and ready to work for it. And no matter how unsure they are about how to realize their dreams, they are willing to face whatever challenges that may lie ahead. Imam Feisal Abdul Rauf is one such voice, brimming with hope, yet founded in history and experience.

These voices urgently require our support in every way possible over these coming years. They must be amplified by every means possible within the Middle East, the larger Muslim world, and in the West as part of a process of transforming the mutual fear and suspicion that define our relations today. This book can be an important tool helping to build a constructive and mutually beneficial dialogue among our related civilizations.

Imam Feisal Abdul Rauf speaks from the heart about a higher ground on which we can all unite. *What's Right with Islam* should be required reading for all people of good will interested in a better tomorrow.

September 16th, 2004

NAIF AL-MUTAWA

"Obsessed with wanting to crack the code, I reread the book looking for some clue."

How many of you read J. D. Salinger's *The Catcher in the Rye* when you were in high school? I remember the novel as if it were yesterday. I became enamored with the writer and went on to read his other novels.

I remember his use of language. I remember the story of protagonist Holden Caulfield who finds the hypocrisy, phoniness, and ugliness of the world around him almost unbearable, and through his cynicism he tries to protect himself from the pain and disappointment of the world. I remember not wanting the story to end; I even remember that I used the book as a way to procrastinate and not write my college essays. I remember all of this.

Yet, funnily enough, I don't remember the urge to shoot a cultural icon. In fact I never had the urge to shoot anyone. Not after reading the book. Not now. Not ever.

Mark David Chapman, the assassin who gunned down Beatle John Lennon on December 9th, 1980, carried with him a copy of J. D. Salinger's *The Catcher in the Rye* and referred to the book during his interrogation by the police. John Hinckley, the would-be assassin of President Ronald Reagan in 1981, was also obsessed with the book. Both of them somehow tied their criminally violent acts to the same book.

Sound familiar?

Obsessed with wanting to crack the code, I reread the book looking for some clue. Clearly there must be something wrong with me that I could not decipher the code in the book. I started reading every other letter to see if there was a pattern. I even held the book up to a mirror and tried to read the book backward. I squinted to look for clues. Frustrated, I flirted with the idea of standing on my hands but the ratio of my height to my weight was not supportive of such a task. At the very least, I thought maybe the rush of blood to my head would help me find something.

I found nothing.

Clearly I was not as inspired as Chapman or Hinckley. I was not chosen for such a message. I was not worthy of the author of those words to be communicating personally and directly to me through his writing.

I was not meant for greater things.

But clearly Chapman was. He married a Japanese woman, like Lennon. He formed a band of four men, like Lennon. He clothed and lived according to his idol. He wanted to be Lennon.

In any and all situations that require interpretation, it is very important to fully understand the cultural context as well as the psychological context of the person interpreting the situation—whether it relates to the written word or otherwise.

People can only relate based on what they do know and frankly, what they are wired to know.

Giving chosen people carte blanche to interpret anything is akin to catastrophe, especially when one then attempts to graft that thought to another time and place.

I asked one of my medical students what kind of doctor he wanted to be. He said surgeon. I was impressed. Later on that day, I asked my five-year-old son Khalid what he wanted to be when he grew up—he said a doctor. When I asked him what kind of doctor he thought for moment and said, "A blue doctor."

Clearly you don't want my little Smurf dictating the course of the future of medicine. However, being a kindergartner in the midst of learning basic categories, his answer was actually as impressive as that of the future surgeon. Each answered according to the resources and options available.

To date, sixty million copies of *The Catcher in the Rye* have been sold and only two violent crimes that I know of have been linked to the book. Clearly the fault is that of the reader.

December 4th, 2010

RAFAEL AMARGO

"Just as I must breathe and I must eat to dance, so too must I read."

I was born to dance. I danced before I walked. I even danced before I was born—at least according to my mother, who swears that I danced in her womb. I suppose she should know because having a flamenco dancer inside of you must not make for an easy pregnancy.

Flamenco for me is a passion. It is my life—my religion; I know nothing else. I dance flamenco because I want to, yes; but, I also dance flamenco because I must. Drama runs through my family like blood courses through veins. Growing up in my house, everyone was very theatrical—always dancing and singing. Everyone still does. It is the way we are as a family of artists—it is how we are happy.

My real name is Jesús Rafael García Hernández, but Rafael Amargo is my stage name. Rafael after my grandfather and Amargo after a poem in the book *Romancero Gitano* by Federico García Lorca.

My grandfather, the patriarch of our family, was a postman by profession. He was postman to Federico García Lorca; but, the relationship between my family and Lorca is much deeper than that, because we are family—Lorca and my grandfather were cousins.

Thus my family and I are Lorquianes. Reading Lorca in my house is not a luxury, a diversion, or a coincidence—it is a sacred duty. The work of Lorca is the major inspiration of my life.

I have read most of Lorca's work again and again. However, I am particularly drawn to *Poeta en Nueva York* (*Poet in New York*). It was his last complete work, which I first read when I was thirteen or fourteen, but only really fully absorbed for its depth and beauty when I was about twenty-two. It is to *Poeta en Nueva York* that I owe the success of my career, because I was fortunate to bring this work through dance to theater with the music of Leonard Cohen.

However, Lorca's work influences me on a daily basis. It never leaves me—it is imprinted on my heart. I often find myself thinking back to a quote from another of his works in which he wrote beautifully, hauntingly, that "to burn with desire and keep quiet about it is the greatest punishment we can bring on ourselves."

Reading teaches and toughens. It builds our minds, it improves our health, it nourishes our souls. Just as I must breathe and I must eat to dance, so too must I read to inform my art about which I "burn with desire."

December 12th, 2016

ANOUSHEH ANSARI

"I would live through the lives of heroes and heroines such as Florence Nightingale and Marie Curie in books, and dream of visiting far-off places—even the stars."

Growing up in Tehran in the late 1960s and 1970s, I didn't have a lot of extracurricular activities, so books were the best gifts I ever received. I learned about the world through books and I spent a lot of time reading. I would live through the lives of heroes and heroines such as Florence Nightingale and Marie Curie in books, and dream of visiting far-off places—even the stars.

I have always loved the stars. Looking up at the night sky as a child, I would dream of flying through space and living on another planet. For as long as I can remember, I believed in the power of dreams.

When I told people I was going to space, they would say, "Oh that's nice." But no one really believed me. No one took me seriously. I was dismissed. Then, one day, at our school library, I came across *Le Petit Prince* (*The Little Prince*) by Antoine de Saint-Exupéry. I fell in love with this book—I loved it as a child and I love it now.

At the time, I was attending a French Catholic school that was in Tehran. So, I initially read it in French.

The Little Prince seemed to speak directly to me. The narrator (the pilot) relates his experience with adults and how he was usually misunderstood by them. The way he saw things was much more imaginative than an adult, and the little prince understood him.

With *The Little Prince* I started thinking more about living in space and going to other planets. Each time I shared my dreams of traveling through space and an adult dismissed me, I thought of the pilot and especially of the little prince who traveled in spite of everyone's skepticism.

As I grew up, this dream of space travel stayed with me. I continued to share my dreams, which continued to be met with skepticism. Even five or six years before I traveled to the space station, I don't think most people really believed I would ever fly to space.

Then on September 18th of 2006, I boarded the Soyuz TMA-9 with the Russian space program, traveling to the International Space Station.

I was in space for eleven days. My mission, especially being on the space station, reminded me of the little prince's planet, which was very small comparatively. The space station was my planet and I could have been the little prince. I had a little area for myself and I could see the earth from my window.

It was like I was looking down at the universe. How could I not reflect on *The Little Prince*, and the little girl in Tehran dreaming of traveling through space, telling people she would go, and seeing the dream come true by gazing back at planet Earth?

I believe that reading *The Little Prince* influenced me deeply and has helped me hold on to those childhood dreams when no one else believed me. I know I am an adult now. But, at heart, I'm still a child. Often because of the way I think of things I'm accused of not acting my age, which I take as the greatest compliment.

I believe that our hope for the world relies on empowering youth and nurturing their imagination—not dismissing them—so that, as they grow up, they can imagine a better world and pursue their dreams by creating one. If we can empower our children and open their minds—through education and reading—and listen to them more, we will be able to create a much brighter, more peaceful future for all.

December 29th, 2016

LAUREN BACALL

"I had never been in a play that was written by a poet, and the prospect filled me with wonder."

As a child, I spent more time dreaming about what I wanted to be rather than being what I was, and reading was the first key to imagining all these different lives and possibilities for my own life. As an actor, reading is the first step into a world and a life that you will inhabit—and that will inhabit you—intimately, for weeks, months, sometimes years.

In 1984, I was offered the part of Alexandra Del Lago, an actress, in Tennessee Williams's *Sweet Bird of Youth*. I had never been in a play that was written by a poet, and the prospect filled me with wonder. What would it be like? I could hardly wait to find out.

Tennessee's words, the torment of him and of his characters, stimulated me. Gradually I found myself living completely within his world. With a playwright like Williams, there is no way to avoid doing so. Onstage I lived so many of the princess's fears, they were intertwined with my own. I found that as I spoke—in this play with its extraordinary and poetic language—the words surrounded me, made me warm and safe, held me up. That kind of writing does almost all the work, and Tennessee was one of the few playwrights in my lifetime who could provide it. He made me feel that I was a better actress. I could be reckless, could let go, I could rise to his occasion. And if not—I could come close. Closer than I ever had before.

June 11th, 2003

KEITH BLACK

"I felt excitement and clarity about what I wanted to do in my life that was, in hindsight, astonishing given my relative youth when I read the book."

The Making of a Surgeon by William A. Nolen, MD, inspired me to become a doctor and a brain surgeon. I came across this book by chance when I was at a bookstore in junior high school.

At the time I had already developed a deep interest in science, which has been an enduring and guiding passion in my life. However, I didn't really know what I wanted to do with my interest in science. We didn't have any physicians in my family, nor did we have any family friends who worked in the profession. Thus, my only real knowledge about the field of medicine prior to reading *The Making of a Surgeon* came from my visits to doctors' offices.

This book opened a whole new world for me. I came to understand the process and the challenges of preparing myself for medical school, residency, and my future career as a doctor. Nolen articulates what it feels like to be a doctor in good times and in bad, through trials and tribulations. His book gave me a glimpse into the world of surgery; and, I felt an excitement and clarity about what I wanted to do in my life that was, in hindsight, astonishing given my relative youth when I read the book.

Many years have passed since I first read *The Making of a Surgeon* and many years have passed since I began my career. Reflecting back, I am struck by just how powerful a role one book can play in the life of an individual. Also, since my specialty is the brain, I am deeply interested in how humans process information.

Reading has always been an important part of my life as a source of knowledge, information, and entertainment. It is also one of the most efficient ways to get new information assimilated into the brain. When we read, our minds create images of what is being described on the page. Those images prove to be powerful tools in creating and retaining memories, because those images may be more creative, enjoyable, and memorable than something we see or hear.

Therefore, when people ask me for parenting advice, I always tell them that they should read to their children and encourage their children to read themselves. This helps to develop an innate sense of curiosity. Reading will also be an endless source of entertainment and knowledge, while helping to improve memory. Ultimately, it can also lead people to an epiphanous book that helps to shape their lives in the way that *The Making of a Surgeon* helped to shape mine.

December 22nd, 2016

T. C. BOYLE

"There is a wild uncontainable genius in these stories."

The book that first awakened me to the wonderfully subversive possibilities of literature is Flannery O'Connor's *The Complete Stories*, which contains wonderfully perverse (and yet rigorously moral) pieces like "A Good Man Is Hard to Find," an apparent situation comedy that turns deeply and shockingly dark, as well as the very bleak comedy of "Good Country People," in which prejudices prove fatal. There is a wild uncontainable genius in these stories that spoke to me and pushed me, however haphazardly, toward essaying my own stories.

May 9th, 2013

GABRIEL BYRNE

"Those early books made me realize that there was another world—a world outside my own—an exotic, exciting and safe world I could travel to whenever I opened a book."

To this day, I can't pass a bookshop without going in. I find books sensual and seductive. I love opening an old Penguin in a secondhand bookshop and losing myself in the yellowing pages.

This love of books permeates my life. There is nothing more comforting in a room than books; I gravitate toward them. I've heard of people who go into other people's houses and snoop through their medicine cabinets, but I snoop through their libraries! I'm intrigued to know books people read. When I see someone reading a book—even a stranger on the street—I can't resist the urge to go up and ask them about it. If they say, "this is an amazing book; you've got to read it," I do.

I grew up outside of Dublin, in the countryside of Ireland, before the advent of television. My mother had a tremendous love of books, education, and learning, which I suppose planted those early seeds. I also remember the old storytellers regaling us with tales and stories, but I found school a fearful place. I was beaten a lot there; we all were. Those were the days of corporal punishment, "spare the rod and spoil the child." So, I never really understood that learning could actually be enjoyable, until I entered one class in primary school.

I no longer remember the teacher's name, but I remember him physically, and I must have been about six or seven when he started reading *Coco's Gold* to us, it was probably a corny book, but he happened to be a really good reader—a good actor I suppose. The book was written in short chapters and he rationed out a chapter a day. I would wake up bursting with excitement to find out what happened next. He slowly but surely addicted us to reading.

The Wind in the Willows by Kenneth Grahame, was next. I fell in love with the book and I've read it many, many times since. That book and its characters became so real to me that I used to walk beside the riverbank in the afternoon, hoping to bump into Mr. Mole, Mr. Rat or, most of all, Mr. Toad in his shiny red motor car.

I find it hard to articulate the excitement I felt at the realization that I could move from one world to another and that I could do this through the pages of books. Those early books made me realize that there was another world—a world outside my own—an exotic, exciting and safe world I could travel to whenever I opened a book.

He also introduced us to the world of Irish fairy tales, staying on just the right side of the truth, by explaining, "I'm not saying I was there exactly, but I know a man who was there and he told me that this is what happened." And so, we all came to know the magical fairy tales of our country, with the lines between fiction and fact blurred so convincingly. We were propelled from the gray, dingy reality of Dublin in the late 1950s, to a world of imagined reality.

Reading *Tír na nÓg* (*Land of the Ever-living*) fascinated me. It is the tale of a young warrior named Oisín who was out hunting in the woods with his friend one day, when they came upon a beautiful girl riding a horse with wings. When Oisín asks where she is from, she says, "I'm from Tír na nÓg, a land beyond the clouds." He goes there with her, on the back of her magical horse, but after what seems like a year in Tír na nÓg, he asks to return to Ireland to visit his family and friends. She allows him to go back on the winged horse, but warns him that he must not set foot on Irish soil. While trying to help some workmen, he falls off the horse and, since many, many decades have passed in Ireland, he shrivels up into an old man and dies.

After he told the story, our teacher pointed out the window of our schoolroom at the hill and told us that it was the very spot where Oisín had seen the beautiful maiden. For weeks after that, we would look out that window and imagine the warrior, the beautiful maiden and her magical, winged horse on top of that hill.

I enjoyed the tale, but as with many stories and books I've read, I didn't really understand the significance of the message until much later. The story is exactly the same, the words are the same, but over time, I find that I understand the message in a different way. *Tír na nÓg* is very powerful because it really tells the tale of the Irish people who, faced with abject poverty at home, emigrated, tearing the heart out of the country. A universal truth, which I have come to know as an adult living between two cultures, is enshrined in that myth. The fable points out that you can go back, but you can never really belong. When I go back to Ireland, I realize how much I love it. At the same time, I realize that I cannot stay and that I have to go back to my own Tír na nÓg, where I am now from—America.

My life, my experience, and the path I have chosen could have been very different without the passion for books and reading instilled in me by one primary school teacher who really cared. I like to think that he was a link in a chain that I am now part of.

I know that I have a passion for reading and I believe that there are people who have taken that passion from me and gone on to read books that I have recommended, from Kenneth Grahame's *The Wind in the Willows*, to Somerset Maugham's *Of Human Bondage*. Some of those people will also reach others, becoming part of a chain that links people through this common bond of reading and books, transmitting a gift beyond measure—curiosity. Which leads to knowledge, which is power.

January 21st, 2004

"It is a book strong enough to change the way we perceive the world."

I was twelve years old in 1957, when the Little Rock School integration crisis burst upon our community in Arkansas. It was all very confusing, because there were competing claims, competing values, conflicting interests, and conflicting opinions. I struggled to understand this crisis, race and change in America, but I wasn't receiving any guidance at home, at school, or at church. Consequently, I couldn't find the right direction, and those issues remained in conflict for me.

Then as a senior in high school, I read Alan Paton's *Cry, the Beloved Country*, the deeply moving story of a Zulu pastor and his son in South Africa. This book is about the problems of race and justice in South Africa, but its message is much bigger than that. It's really about the problems of humanity—it's about the meaning of civilization and how we move forward with the organization of promoting the values we cherish. Those values aren't the property of any particular country, culture, race, creed, or sect.

In my opinion, *Cry, the Beloved Country* reaches the heart not only of the issues; it reaches the heart and emotions of those who read it. It is a book strong enough to change the way we perceive the world. For me, it provided an intellectual and emotional foundation for breaking free of the conflicts in my culture and community, which helped me find my way forward in my own beliefs.

The year after I read *Cry, the Beloved Country*, I left Arkansas to attend the Military Academy of West Point. It was my first time dealing with a different culture—a meritocracy in which everyone was treated as an equal. They didn't care who your parents were, or how much money you had. They didn't care what kind of car you drove. No one drove a car. They didn't care who you dated. There were no women to date. Everyone was treated equally regardless of race, religion, or background, and everyone was expected to perform. The only thing that mattered was who you were and what you believed in.

Cry, the Beloved Country had unlocked an understanding in me. This understanding helped me to set aside the conflict that had been ingrained in me by my upbringing in Arkansas and thrive in an environment like West Point.

Wes Clark

January 17th, 2003

HIS HOLINESS THE DALAI LAMA

"When I am reading I am often reminded of the great
kindness of the scholars and translators of the past."

It sometimes surprises me that there is so much talk about the right to freedom of speech, but much less about the right to freedom to read, perhaps because we take it so much for granted. For hundreds of years reading and access to books have been fundamental to extending our knowledge and education. Reading books allows us to learn more about the world in which we live, but also more about the people we share it with, the way they think and the experiences they have.

As a Buddhist monk my main education—as well as the majority of the books I have read—have been concerned with Buddhist thought and practice. The primary object of the Buddha's teachings is to enable people to transform their minds, which can only be effectively achieved if the instructions are conveyed in a language that the reader can understand.

Therefore, when I am reading I am often reminded of the great kindness of the scholars and translators of the past who translated a vast array of Buddhist literature into Tibetan. Over the course of several centuries, small teams working together made books available to Tibetans that allowed a deep understanding of the Buddha's teachings to take root in Tibet. It was this understanding that later found expression in the many books composed by Tibetan authors. Hence, it gives me great pleasure to know that there are experienced translators today working steadily to translate Buddhist books from Tibetan into English, which will undoubtedly make an invaluable contribution to a deep and lasting understanding of the Buddhist tradition in Western lands.

I first learned to read at about the age of seven and have valued books ever since. Now, I'm eighty-one years old but, whenever I have free time, I read. I believe that reading books can help us make this life meaningful. Therefore, I am very happy to learn that the proceeds of this book, *The World is Just a Book Away*, will purchase books and build libraries for children who have none. My greetings to all the children and students who will benefit from this project. I hope you will not only find the books you want, but will also discover and take interest in others you would otherwise not have known about.

December 8th, 2016

SHOBHAA DÉ

"I don't regret smoking awful cigarettes inside shabby local cafes and imagining I was Simone de Beauvoir."

As a little girl growing up in New Delhi and later, in Mumbai, I discovered Enid Blyton decades before I stumbled upon the great Indian epic, the *Mahabharata*. Sounds absurd, right? I guess it was pretty insane that a six-year-old daughter of a senior bureaucrat would routinely disappear into a world of English schools, tuck shops, and scones, a world that was so far removed from her "heat and dust" reality. But I did! Enid Blyton . . . and Heidi! Johanna Spyri created *Heidi* in 1881. How I adored Heidi and her grandfather. My fascination with Heidi, the girl from the Alps, a Swiss orphan, may have had something to do with the fact I'd lost both my grandfathers before I was born. But I yearned for a kindly old man, who would take care of me, and let me play with wooly lambs. I still dream I am Heidi, lying on a bed of straw and calling out to my dear grandpa.

That is the magic of books. We can dive into worlds that are so distant, and so unfamiliar . . . and make them our own. We occupy them effortlessly . . . live in them—vividly and passionately, because our imagination allows us to.

By the time I started reading "real" books about "real" people, my mind had been conditioned and trained to look for and recognize richness—of language, plot, characters. Most of the childlike wonder I'd experienced identifying with Heidi and her magical life, had been replaced by awareness of a more self-conscious adult variety. I fell in love with Prince Andrei. I became Natasha. I wanted to elope with Anatole. Learn the art of seduction from Hélène. And marry Pierre. *War and Peace* took over my life completely.

I still hadn't discovered the *Mahabharata*.

Today, I think, isn't that odd? Why did I ignore my own, exceptionally rich literature and focus on say, Russian writers in translation? Why Leo Tolstoy? Why not Rabindranath Tagore? Why wasn't I reading his *Gitanjali* and admiring the fluid imagery of India's Nobel laureate? How come nobody in my school or college nudged me to read books in my mother tongue—Marathi? Why were my parents giving Jane Austen and Emily Brontë (God bless their souls) novels to me and not the works of Indian writers?

So many decades later, I have still a great deal of catching up to do . . . with my own . . . about my own.

And no, I don't regret smoking awful cigarettes inside shabby local cafes and imagining I was Simone de Beauvoir. Or crying while reading *Bonjour tristesse*. Albert Camus? He was my best friend. F. Scott Fitzgerald, too. *Tender is the Night*, with its evocative opening lines, became my sanctuary. I thought Zelda was utterly cool, and wondered whether I would end up like her . . . or Sylvia Plath. It was a foolish time in my life when suicidal thoughts were considered mandatory if you wanted to belong.

I still hadn't attempted the *Mahabharata*.

After intensifying my reading to include German philosophers and Caribbean poets, I drifted a bit aimlessly and pointlessly toward Germaine Greer and Gloria Steinem. I was looking for validation and freedom. I didn't find it there. Then, Toni Morrison happened. Alice Walker and Angela Davis too. Much later, along came Ben Okra and upset my world yet again. I realized it was important for books to disrupt and unsettle my mind from time to time. Or else, I'd take them and the writers for granted. Worse, I'd take *myself* for granted. And I would become a bit too easy to please . . . complacent. Books, I concluded rather loftily and grandly, were obliged to create ripples and waves inside one's heart.

So . . . I am glad I met the *Mahabharata* when I did, when I had to.

For it was the right time to meet Krishna.

A more complex and irresistible man has yet to be written. Krishna ("My opulence is limitless") made me feel powerless . . . breathless . . . recharged. His priceless advice to Arjuna just before the great battle, remains the perfect philosophical treatise of all time. Cunning, shrewd, tactical, and tender, Krishna as he is depicted in the *Gita*, is Everyman . . . and every God. Clearing cosmic confusion and showing the way to Arjuna, a warrior who finds himself confronting several moral dilemmas, Krishna becomes the fearless charioteer of Arjuna's mind . . . and leads him to victory. There is tragedy embedded in the win. But that's another story.

These days, I turn to Krishna. Strange. I find myself in him. Maybe Krishna is Everywoman, too.

December 7th, 2016

SHIRIN EBADI

"People might be surprised to learn that I have found great inspiration in the autobiography of an American cyclist."

Violence is part of my everyday life, because my work is on the violation of human rights. Each day, I encounter stories of violence that weigh heavily on my mind and each day I tell myself, "you don't have the right to get tired," because I also know that the day I don't fight or the day I don't work, I will have nothing left to do.

At times I don't know where I will get the energy to continue my work, but I know I must. To be able to sleep at night, I try to read a little—it might be anything from literature and poetry, to novels and biographies. These books are a vital part of my life because they are entertaining, relaxing, and educating to me, which does give me inspiration and energy.

I read mostly in Persian and throughout my life, I have read most of the great Persian authors and poets. Currently, most of the books I read tend to be books written in other languages and translated into Persian. Lately, I find myself especially drawn to biographies and autobiographies of great men and women who have overcome adversity through the ages to persevere and triumph. I find the fact that human beings can be so strong in the face of such adversity very beautiful.

Recently, I read *It's Not About the Bike: My Journey Back to Life*, by Lance Armstrong. At first, given my life's work, people might be surprised to learn that I have found great inspiration in the autobiography of an American cyclist. And yet I have. I find his will to succeed, his courage, and his sheer determination to live extremely inspirational.

When Lance Armstrong, at what seemed the height of his career, discovered that he had lung and brain cancer with about a 50/50 chance of survival, he was devastated. Many people would have relinquished hope and resigned themselves to a perceived fate. But, instead—and much to his credit—Lance Armstrong chose to fight back. Essentially, he said to his cancer, "you have chosen a bad body to afflict. I'm going to fight you." And, he did, with an aggressive treatment program that proved successful. The rest, as they say, is history, with Lance Armstrong going on to become a world hero, winning a record-breaking seven *Tour de France* races and, in 2008, being named one of *Time Magazine*'s "100 Most Influential People."

Today Lance Armstrong says that the cancer was the best thing that ever happened to him. He launched the Lance Armstrong Foundation and is a world leader in the fight against cancer. I like to think about his story and relate his story because it is so illustrative of the choices we can make in life. Yes, when faced with seemingly insurmountable odds—whether they be related to health or the violation of our basic human rights—we can give up. We can accept our "fate" or the unethical behavior of others toward us. Or, as hard as it may be and as impossible as it may seem, we can choose to stand up and fight.

Lance Armstrong chose to stand up and fight for his health and his life. He translated his journey into an international battle against cancer that is changing the life of millions. His autobiography really isn't about his life as an athlete. Instead, it's about his journey as a human being and his determination to triumph no matter what the circumstances. This is why I find such inspiration in *It's Not About the Bike: My Journey Back to Life*.

November 4th, 2009

DANIEL ELLSBERG

"I would be happy if the words I read aloud that morning in 2004, after my own short night in jail, reached the hearts of some young listeners and changed their lives as they had mine, a quarter-century earlier."

"How does it become a man to behave toward this American government today? I answer, that he cannot without disgrace be associated with it."
—Henry David Thoreau, *On the Duty of Civil Disobedience*

In the fall of 2002, I was using my book tour for *Secrets: A Memoir of Vietnam and the Pentagon Papers* to warn people that we were being lied into war, just as we had been with the Tonkin Gulf, which was described in the first chapter of my book. The world's opposition to a US attack on Iraq—which, in the absence of UN authorization, was a blatant crime against peace, an active act of aggression—was evident with the protest of as many as ten million people in cities around the world on February 15th, 2003. This was the largest global protest the world had ever seen. Nonetheless, the administration moved forward and the "shock and awe" campaign—the bombing of Baghdad—was scheduled to begin on March 19th, 2003.

I knew it would begin with very heavy bombing, intended to not only paralyze resistance, but also to terrorize the population into subservience. The very idea of this was appalling to me—almost unbearable. I was in Washington, DC, at the time and a group named Code Pink, mainly comprised of women, had scheduled an act of disobedience in front of the White House. At the last minute, I decided to join this protest and join the people lying on the street surrounded by police.

We were all arrested and hogtied. Our wrists were essentially handcuffed to our ankles with plastic cuffs. Through the years, I had been arrested some seventy times, but I had never been hogtied. This was apparently a new method the police were practicing for use against terrorists.

We were asked to sign a citation for immediate release, meaning that we would come back for a later trial and perhaps pay a small fine. I imagined my release and being in the outside world where I would simply be unable to bear watching the bombing on television. I knew I would either be tempted to watch it, in pain, or feel that I was evading it. At that moment, I was struck by the thought that I was exactly where I wanted to be as a citizen of this government at that time—in jail.

Passages from H. D. Thoreau's essay originally titled *On Resistance to Civil Government* and later published as *On the Duty of Civil Disobedience* came to mind as I sat there. I remembered him stating something to the effect that the true place for a just man when his government is acting unjustly is prison. I felt that my government was acting unjustly and that being in a jail cell, for protesting the aggression, was the right place not to watch it.

Everyone else did sign, agreeing to pay a fine. One by one, they were released until I was the last person in the jail. My refusal to sign puzzled the police, and when the processor asked me why I refused to leave, at first I didn't give an explanation; I just stated that I didn't choose to. A little later, asked by another officer, I remarked that I didn't want to watch my country bombing Baghdad on television. He said, "Oh, we'll put you in with the general jail population, where the TV will be on all the time." Blackmail. But I went ahead with the booking anyway.

When they moved me, alone, to another jail downtown, the young officer who handcuffed me to the police van asked why I was staying in. "Can't you afford the bail?" I said I could, but I preferred to be inside. He asked why, and I said. "Well, I read a book." I asked him if he'd ever heard of Henry Thoreau and he said, "no." Somehow I wasn't surprised. I told him that it would be a good thing for him to read Thoreau's essay *On the Duty of Civil Disobedience*, and he said he would. I hope he has.

They didn't carry out their threat to put me in a room with TV. I got my own cell, nothing in it but a metal toilet and a metal slab of a cot, without a mattress. I lay on it with my shoes for a pillow and thought: Perfect.

I tried to recall some of Thoreau's exact words from his night in jail. It was only one night, because his aunt paid the fine. This was much to his displeasure, because he had hoped to force a trial, where he could make an open protest against the Mexican War and the institution of slavery.

Although I intended to stay in jail over the weekend, a friend of mine, Peter Kuznick of American University, who had organized a teach-in for the next morning to protest the attack, got a call through to me in the middle of the night—the sergeant brought a cellphone to my cell—and urged me strongly to come out. They had advertised my participation to the students, and he was counting on me as a main speaker. I told him I really preferred to stay in. In fact, I thought that was the best statement I could make to students.

(As Thoreau had put it, I read again the next morning, "If any think that their influence would be lost there [in jail], and their voices no longer afflict the ear of the state . . . they do not know by how much truth is stronger than error, nor how much more eloquently and effectively he can combat injustice who has experienced a little in his own person.")

Earlier that evening, as we waited to be booked, I had asked another protestor who was also hogtied, six feet from where I was bound (another antiterrorist precaution) but who planned to sign out, to call Peter and tell him I would be unable to be present in person at the teach-in. I said, "Tell him I'm in a secure location." Kuznick had heard this message with dismay. He got a lawyer friend, Jack Baringer, to find out where I was being held and get through to me, saying he was representing me. I was reluctant to leave the cell. The shock and awe had more than another day to go—but he finally persuaded me, on Peter's behalf, to honor my earlier commitment and make my statement in person at the teach-in. After I signed the paper for the local sergeant, he insisted that I leave the jail through the outer door immediately. He was not friendly to our cause. He told me he had served in Vietnam, as I had, I told him, which didn't impress him, and he refused to let me call the lawyer to ask him to pick me up. I was now free, on a dark corner somewhere in DC at four in the morning without a belt or shoelaces (suicide risks), a jacket, wallet, ID, or spare change. All of these things were somewhere at the police training center in Virginia where we had been booked. I had no idea where I was, and I didn't know if the lawyer did either, but after a while Baringer did turn up in his car.

By the time we retrieved my belongings it was morning, and we headed for American University. But on the way, still thinking of Thoreau, I went to the library in Cleveland Park and checked out a copy of Thoreau's essay. I wanted to check my memory, and perhaps find an apt passage for the students.

I found the specific passage I'd thought of after my arrest, which went, "Under a government which imprisons any unjustly, the true place for a just man is also a prison." The words were a little different than I had remembered, because I wasn't protesting slavery, like Thoreau. Though I might as well have been since Abu Ghraib lay ahead and Guantanamo and secret CIA prison cells had been operating for over a year. I was protesting a wrongful war, just like Thoreau (in his case the then-ongoing Mexican War.) I had learned, not long before, that President Polk had not only deliberately provoked an alleged attack on American forces—like the Tonkin Gulf incidents I had observed from the Pentagon—but had also lied the country into an aggressive war as blatantly as LBJ had done in Vietnam and now Bush in Iraq. I read in the car, as we drove to American University, words that rang like a trumpet call:

> When a sixth of the population of a nation which has undertaken to be the refuge of liberty are slaves, and a whole country is unjustly overrun and conquered by a foreign army, and subjected to military law, I think that it is not too soon for honest men to rebel and revolutionize. What makes this duty the more urgent is the fact that the country overrun is not our own, but ours is the invading army.

To find myself reading this while, at that very moment, American bombers were blasting the capital of a country that had neither attacked nor threatened us, was uncanny. And as I read on, I found many passages so astonishingly relevant to what was going on that morning—and still is going on, horribly, four years later—that I felt called on when we arrived to spend most of my scheduled time simply quoting from this book. Commentary was hardly needed that morning, still less four years later.

Even the references to slavery have become increasingly apt. In 2006 the congress of a country that had undertaken to be a refuge of liberty passed the Military Commissions Act, which reduces the rights to zero of alien residents in this country singled out by the president, or those acting in his name. If the executive branch identifies them as enemies, or suspects, or supporters of organizations it designates as terrorist, they have, under this act, no right to not be detained without showing cause; no right of habeas corpus, appeal to a judge to rule on their detention; no right to not be detained indefinitely without counsel and without appeal, in what amounts to a gulag in this country and its cooperating allies; no right not to be tortured (by whatever name), nor even, not to be tortured to death. In short, their rights can be determined by the president to be the rights of slaves: nonexistent. No rights that an American president or anyone serving him is bound to respect. As if they were civilians in Iraq.

I read to the students, that morning in March 2003:

> There are thousands who are *in opinion* [Thoreau's emphasis] opposed to slavery and to the war, who yet in effect do nothing to put an end to them . . . They hesitate, and they regret, and sometimes they petition, but they do nothing in earnest and with effect. They will wait well disposed, for others to remedy the evil, that they may no longer have it to regret. At most they give only a cheap vote . . .

And this:

> The soldier is applauded who refuses to serve in an unjust war by those who do not refuse to sustain [by their tax money] the unjust government which makes the war.

Applauded? Well, by some in the antiwar movement of which I am part. But also prosecuted like Lt. Ehren Watada, on trial for being the single officer in the armed services to take seriously his oath to protect and defend the Constitution in refusing to deploy to an unjust war—or Sgt. Camilo Mejia, who served his country better during his nine months in prison for refusing to return to Iraq than he did in his previous tour there.

And meanwhile, these courageous patriots are *emulated* by hardly anyone. Republicans and Democrats alike in the House and the Senate who state publicly that the president's course of action is hopeless and must change or end, have proceeded to use their votes to fund his "surge" to the limits of his requests. To cutting off the funding—which is their constitutional power to end the war, if they would use it—they do not give even a cheap vote. And those who do, on funding resolutions that they know the president will veto, go no further.

They do not act by and large with admirable exceptions to obstruct the president's programs or other funding, or by filibusters (routinely used by Republicans to maintain the war), or to investigate the many high crimes and misdemeanors of the administration that would lead to impeachments of the president and vice president and criminal prosecutions of them and many of their subordinates. Nor do those who voted them into office openly commit themselves to turning them out of office if they continue to ignore their own constitutional powers and duties— their own oaths to protect and defend the Constitution.

In short, all of these citizens fail to heed Thoreau's ringing advice below, which changed my life when I first read it in 1969, shortly before I encountered young Americans who were consciously acting on it, and on the example of Thoreau's heirs, Gandhi and Martin Luther King, Jr.:

> Let your life be a counter friction to stop the machine. What I have to do is to see, at any rate, that I do not lend myself to the wrong which I condemn . . . Cast your whole vote, not a strip of paper merely, but your whole influence. A minority is powerless while it conforms to the majority; it is not even a minority then; but it is irresistible when it clogs by its whole weight.

It was the example in 1969 of young draft resisters who were casting their whole vote—like Watada, like Mejia—by accepting prosecution and imprisonment rather than to participate in what they, and I, perceived to be a wrongful war. That challenged me to find a way to cast my own whole vote. One way I thought of was to copy and give Congress and the press the seven-thousand-page top secret study of Vietnam decision making—a record of the lies, deceptions, and crimes of four administrations—that became known as the Pentagon Papers.

I didn't go to prison on that occasion—though I had expected to, for life—because my twelve-count federal indictment, with a possible sentence of 115 years, was dismissed after four months in court on grounds of governmental criminal misconduct against me during my two years under indictment. But my action, with the help of my friend and codefendant Tony Russo, my wife Patricia, and many others, proved to be a useful thing to do. Though, like anything else, its impact wasn't permanent.

If I had been convicted and served a full sentence, I would be getting out, with good behavior, in 2008 to find my country once again mired in a brutal, hopeless, criminal war. The lessons of Vietnam and the Pentagon Papers have not been studied or followed in recent years, not by the executive, Congress, the media, or the voters. Yet they are, in fact, still relevant, and will be again like the timeless lessons of the essay, *On the Duty of Civil Disobedience*. I would be happy if the words I read aloud that morning in 2003, after my own short night in jail, reached the hearts of some young listeners and changed their lives as they had mine, a quarter-century earlier.

As for officials whose hearts and ears might be open to his message, Thoreau's advice to any public officer who might ask him, "But what shall I do?" was "If you really wish to do anything, resign your office." I would say something beyond that to officials who might be in the position that I was in 1964, knowing with inside access and documents that the president was lying the country into a wrongful and disastrous war.

"Don't just resign, quietly," I have been saying to such officials as might hear me over the last five years, ever since the approach to the attack on Iraq, beginning a few months before the shock and awe and my talk to the students. "When you leave, take a drawerful of incriminating documents with you. Don't wait to disclose them till the bombs have started falling (next, in Iran?) and thousands more have died. Consider doing what I wish I had done in 1964-1965, years before I did; telling the truth to Congress, the press, and the public, with documents, *before* the war. The personal risks to your career, even risks of prison, will be great, but you have the power, at that stage, to save a war's worth of lives."

November 16th, 2007

JANE FONDA

"It showed me that transformation was possible . . . even for me."

The Autobiography of Malcolm X was one of the first books that was an epiphany in my life. I read it in the summer of 1968—a tumultuous time. There were major, tectonic shifts happening all over the world, including the Tet Offensive in Vietnam. The civil rights movement was also in full swing, but I had not been a part of it. I did not even know many African Americans beyond those I had worked with in film—particularly those I met on a film called *Hurry Sundown.*

While making this film, I heard about the Black Nationalist Movement from African Americans. They also told me that the civil rights movement was showing Blacks that the Liberal Democratic establishment didn't dare upset their Southern Dixiecrat brethren by really enforcing desegregation and voting rights laws.

Around that time someone recommended that I read *The Autobiography of Malcolm X* to gain a better understanding of the challenges faced by African Americans. I took it with me to St. Tropez—a rather hedonistic, privileged vacation environment in 1968—where my first husband, Roger Vadim, and I were spending the summer.

I knew that my life was undergoing powerful changes that would probably necessitate my leaving my husband and my life in France. I didn't know what the changes would mean, but I was scared, and I was pregnant. I was seven-months pregnant with a child and I was also pregnant with myself, although I didn't realize it at the time.

Throughout the summer, I tried to escape from all the parties and other events on land by getting into an inflatable raft. I would float out in the water of the Mediterranean and I would read. It was on that raft on the Mediterranean that I read *The Autobiography of Malcolm X.*

This book changed me on many levels. First of all, it provided me—for the first time in my life, with a keyhole through which I could look at the realities of Black life in the United States. I then realized just how little I understood that world, which was so different from mine. I remember in particular Malcolm's description of putting lye on his head to straighten his hair—burning lye that seared into his scalp before he stuck his head in the toilet to wash it out. He went through that horrendous experience just so that he would look the way he thought he should.

He also described being not just denied opportunities that were there for young white people, but being discouraged from even thinking about seeking those opportunities. He saw himself perhaps as a lawyer, but a teacher said, "Are you kidding?" In other words, he was actively discouraged from pursuing that positive path in life.

Instead, he pursued a very different path that led him from where he grew up to Harlem, where he became a numbers-running junkie. His name was Malcolm

Little then and he was kind of lowlife gangster and pimp—a hustler. He seemed to be someone you would easily write off, someone who would never amount to anything, someone who would never matter in the scheme of things.

Then, and this is probably the most profound part of it for me, I remember experiencing with him a very gradual transformation. First he became a Muslim—a radical Muslim—and cleaned up his act. That this religion and this spiritual transformation could motivate him to so profoundly change his life is amazing. Unfortunately, however, it also led him to develop an extremely hostile attitude toward white people. For him at that time white meant bad, white meant racist, white meant danger. That was when he gained his notoriety as a man who advocated violence against whites—a persona that, from the media point of view at least, never left him.

But then, most important of all, is his description of another transformation he experienced through his journey to Mecca. At the holy place of Muslims, he discovered that white people were not racist, because white people from around the world viewed him as a brother. That was when he realized that it was a state of mind that needed to be changed, not the color white.

Reading about Malcolm X's final transformation struck me to my core, because it showed me how deep a transformation could be. This was important for me. It showed me that transformation was possible . . . even for me. I didn't know that I could until I read his book.

After that, I thought a lot about state-of-mind versus the color white and I wondered what kind of white I was. I didn't know because I'd never been challenged. I'd never developed relationships with African Americans and I knew that would have to change if I were to discover the answer. I didn't think I was racist, but as I said, I'd never been tested. Malcolm X's book made me want to be tested.

It was like a sprout that began to grow. It wasn't cognitive at the time, it was somatic, but *The Autobiography of Malcolm X*, together with the Tet Offensive and *The Village of Ben Suc*, by Jonathan Schell, led me to want to come back to America to join the movement. I wanted to make it better. I wanted to make a difference.

October 23rd, 2005

FRANK GEHRY

"I've always wanted to learn, to enjoy the trip to the party as much as the party itself, and Proust opened this insight about living in the moment for me at a late age."

I often find things that interest me unfold like a cat with a ball of thread. You push it and it falls. If you follow it, you always get somewhere. This is true with my work—I'm not sure exactly where it's going when I start, but I always get somewhere. If, however, you deny the thought that sparked your interest because you think, "that's a silly thing to think about right now," you lose that opportunity or that journey. So, when something catches my interest, I don't call it "silly," and I don't dismiss it—I just go with it. This has led me down many interesting paths in life, from architecture, to the sculpture of Claus Sluter, to the books I read.

I don't consider myself particularly literary, but I've always read. I suppose, like most boys of my generation, I read mysteries like the *Hardy Boys* and adventure stories like *Twenty Thousand Leagues under the Sea*. Between the ages of ten and twelve, I was really captivated by *Robinson Crusoe*, which I must have read fifty times. Perhaps it was the element of escapism that attracted me to it. At seventy-eight, I often feel like there is a lot I don't remember. But, I do remember how much I enjoyed reading and how much I enjoyed books.

In Canada, where I grew up, literature was an important part of school curriculum. We studied great poets and writers from Sir Walter Scott and Joseph Conrad, to Shakespeare, Proust, and Joyce. I can't say I always enjoyed the required reading. Reading Joyce in high school was more like doing penance than pleasure—but these great works affected me and something about them has always stayed with me.

In the ensuing years, as my career progressed in architecture, I was more involved with the world of art, architecture, and growing as an architect. In the past ten years, I've become more relaxed and gravitated back to the classics of literature.

In that time, I have read Anthony Trollope, Marcel Proust, and James Joyce. I've been drawn to each of these authors for a different reason. Trollope's books deal with issues discussed in his nineteenth-century English settings, which very much resemble the same issues we're talking about today. Proust, on the other hand, has unique talent to almost deify the trivia of life. His books, such as—*Remembrance of Things Past*—show us that the incidental things, meeting someone, having coffee, or talking with your grandmother—these fleeting moments in a day are so important to our lives. I think we all have a tendency to live for the next moment, instead of the moment we're in. I've always wanted to learn, to enjoy the trip to the party as much as the party itself, and Proust opened this insight about living in the moment for me at a late age.

And then there is Joyce. James Joyce was, in my opinion, the first rapper. This might seem like an odd statement and it would probably surprise most rap aficionados.

A client of mine, the rapper Jay-Z, was seated next to me at a dinner one evening. I knew nothing about rap and I didn't really know what to say to a rapper, so I asked him who the first rapper was. He proceeded to rattle off a list of people I'd never heard of.

Coincidentally, around that time I was listening to Joyce reading *Finnegans Wake*, as a book on CD. There was an actual recording of Joyce's voice in full stream of consciousness mode. Listening to Joyce sounded like my limited experience with rap. After Jay-Z told me who he thought the first rapper was, I presumed to tell him it was James Joyce.

When I returned to Los Angeles, I sent Jay-Z the complete collection of Joyce. I'm not sure I convinced him that Joyce was the first rapper, but the idea intrigued him.

This discussion on rap put me back with *Ulysses*, this time on CD. Every once in a while, he dips into the church liturgy, quoting Latin and prayers from the Catholic Church, which sounded similar to Joyce's stream of consciousness and similar to rap.

I continue to follow balls of thread in life. As a result, the same curiosity that led me to Trollope, Proust, and Joyce, hopefully will lead me on many other adventures and to more great books.

July 7th, 2007

MIEP GIES

"When I read the last word, I didn't feel the pain I'd anticipated. I was glad I'd read it at last."

Mr. Frank was approached with the idea of permitting the diary to be translated and published abroad. He was against it at first, but then he succumbed to the pressure on him to allow the diary a more widespread audience.

Again and again, he'd say to me, "Miep, you must read Anne's writing. Who would have imagined what went on in her quick little mind?" Otto was never discouraged by my continuing refusal. He would always wait awhile and then ask me again.

Finally, I gave in to his insistence. I said, "All right, I will read the diary, but only when I'm totally alone."

The next time I was totally alone, on a warm day, I took the second printing of the diary, went to my room, and shut the door.

With awful fear in my heart, I opened the book and turned to the first page. And so I began to read.

I read the whole diary without stopping. From the first word, I heard Anne's voice come back to speak to me from where she had gone. I lost track of time, Anne's voice tumbled out of the book, so full of life, moods, curiosity, feelings. She was no longer gone and destroyed. She was alive again in my mind.

I read to the very end. I was surprised by how much had happened in hiding that I'd known nothing about. Immediately, I was thankful that I hadn't read the diary after the arrest, during the final nine months of the occupation, while it had stayed in my desk drawer right beside me every day. Had I read it, I would have had to burn the diary, because it would have been too dangerous for people about whom Anne had written.

When I read the last word, I didn't feel the pain I'd anticipated. I was glad I'd read it at last. The emptiness in my heart was eased. So much had been lost, but now Anne's voice would never be lost. My young friend had left a remarkable legacy to the world.

But always, every day of my life, I've wished that things had been different. That even had Anne's diary been lost to the world, Anne and the others might somehow have been saved.

Not a day goes by that I do not grieve for them.

Miep Gies

May 3rd, 2009

JANE GOODALL

"Sometimes I don't know how the ceilings stand the weight of all those books, but I wouldn't change it for the world."

"If things go wrong, if you're disappointed, or if you're really sad, just curl up with a book. In a few minutes, you can be in another world and forget the things that are bothering you in this one. When you finish the book, you'll feel refreshed and renewed." I think there is real wisdom in those words, which my mother spoke so often, and books have been a great comfort to me throughout my life.

I so loved books as a child that I often had trouble tearing myself away from whatever I was reading. When my family sat down to a meal together, we talked. If a question arose at mealtime that no one could answer, someone would get the encyclopedia to look it up. Other than that, we had to put aside whatever book we were reading before each meal. Sunday lunch, however, was an exception. It was a very special time in our house, because we were allowed to read at the table.

Sitting at the table with a book, curling up in front of the fire with a book, taking a book up into the top of my favorite tree, reading under the bedclothes at night when I was supposed to have my light out—I grew up in an atmosphere of books. Although I can't recall the first book I read, I distinctly recall the first book that made a terrific impact on me.

I must have been about seven when I found a copy of *Doctor Doolittle* by Hugh Lofting at the local library, checked it out, and read it three times in one week. As the due date came nearer, I just couldn't bear to have it go back. The night before I had to return it, I stayed up late, reading with my torch under the bedclothes. The following Christmas my grandmother, who knew how much I loved the story, gave me a copy. I can still remember the thrill of opening that parcel.

Doctor Doolittle fed into my passion for animals. He learns to speak animal languages from Polynesia, the parrot, who educates him to be very observant: Watch how a dog twitches his nose and pay attention to how a horse flicks his ear. These things are actually terribly important for anyone studying animal behavior. I found it magical then and I still find it magical today.

In that first book, Dr. Doolittle takes circus animals back to Africa, where they have many adventures. I believe that this sparked my passion for Africa. I read all the other *Doctor Doolittle* books after that and I continued to dream of that far-off continent, which was home to all of those wonderful animals.

By the age of ten, I was in love with Tarzan, and I read the entire Edgar Rice Burroughs *Tarzan* series. We didn't have a lot of money, but when the Johnny Weissmuller *Tarzan* film was released, my mother bought us tickets, which was a huge treat. However, we were only in the cinema for a short time before I burst into loud, noisy tears, so noisy that my mother had to take me outside.

"Whatever is the matter," she asked?

"It wasn't Tarzan," I blurted.

I had read every description of Tarzan in my books and built up a mental image. Johnny Weissmuller did not match up to that image! Today, it is hard for children to imagine a world without television, unless they live in rural areas of the developing world, and they don't have books either. For most children, the mental pictures they have of characters they may read about in books will be those presented to them on TV. The Disney version of Aladdin or Snow White will replace images based on the fairy stories, and James Bond will have the face of Pierce Brosnan or Sean Connery.

I think it's sad that in this era of television and the internet, a child's imagination doesn't necessarily have the free reign it had when I was a child. Children today often prefer websites to books. It's understandable, we move on, but for me there is nothing that can take the place of a good book. After all, you can't very well curl up in bed with a website.

Nonetheless, I think if you spend time reading to children they are likely to develop a love of books. I read to my grandchildren as I read to my son and as my mother read to me. I used to read *The Wind in the Willows* to my son. I also read *The Lord of the Rings* to him when he was much too young to fully appreciate it, but he still enjoyed the story. My grandchildren love the Narnia books, *The Lion, the Witch and the Wardrobe*, and all the others. I read to them whenever I have a chance.

To this day, whether I am in England, America, or anywhere else in the world, I can't go to sleep without reading something, a chapter, a half a chapter, or just a few pages. It is a constant in my life. I very much enjoy reading in my bath. The only trouble is that I am often so tired at the end of a busy day (I'm on the road three hundred days a year) that I often doze off: many of my books are distorted, with wrinkled pages dried by a hotel hair dryer! At Gombe, I sometimes read in bed with a candle under the mosquito net. I have to be very, very careful not to fall asleep!

After *Doctor Doolittle* and *Tarzan*, many other books, from the works of Shakespeare and Keats, to the Bible have moved me or touched me and continue to do so. However, Rachel Carson's *Silent Spring* was truly a seminal book in my life, because of its message about the environment. It was the first book that laid out what we are doing to the environment. The title refers to the springs getting quieter, and quieter, and quieter as the birds and insects die from chemical pesticides and fertilizers. It is a beautifully written book, and it was way ahead of its time. Only recently, some thirty years or so after its first publication, has there been widespread acceptance of her message.

Raising awareness about the environment and protecting animals are central missions in my life, and I travel the world speaking about these topics. Although my schedule only permits me to spend a few weeks a year in England, I always enjoy going back to our house, partly because it is filled with the books of five generations. We have books from my mother's childhood, books my uncle collected, like the early encyclopedias in which we used to look up questions raised at the dinner table, the well-worn copy of *Doctor Doolittle* that my grandmother gave me for Christmas so long ago, and many others. Sometimes I don't know how the ceilings stand the weight of all those books, but I wouldn't change it for the world.

I like the look of books, I like the feel of books, and I like the smell of books. I simply cannot imagine a world without them, because they take me into other worlds. They are sources of knowledge, of comfort, of inspiration, and perhaps most importantly, they are sources of hope.

Jane Goodall

November 6th, 2003

PRESIDENT
MIKHAIL GORBACHEV

"The Russian classics teach us to think, to observe reality,
to value humanity, and to be humane."

When I am asked which politician or philosopher had the greatest influence on me, I find it difficult to make a choice. In the great treasury of world culture it is difficult to single out one person for admiration and devotion.

Yet, I have given thought to this question. I concluded that what influenced me the most was the great Russian literature—the poetry of Pushkin and Lermontov, the novels of Turgenev, Tolstoy, and Dostoyevsky, Chekhov's stories . . . the Russian classics teach us to think, to observe reality, to value humanity, and to be humane.

The habit of reading, acquired in childhood, has remained part of my life ever since. In the years of my youth, when young people were inspired by the idea of building a just society, I read and reread Nikolay Ostrovsky's novel *How the Steel Was Tempered*. During the years of perestroika we were enthralled by Kirghiz writer Chingiz Aitmatov's book, written in Russian, *The Day Lasts More Than a Hundred Years*.

The books by the classics of world literature—Goethe, Charles Dickens, Victor Hugo—also made a great impact on me.

I wish young people to find their place in life, to do good—and make sure you read! Nothing will ever replace books. The world's literature has an abundance of masterpieces. Perhaps it is right that everyone first has to absorb the literature of one's own nation. But I would like to wish that young readers make time for Russian literature as well. Its great virtues are profound thought and the moral message. I am convinced this is something people will always need.

January 12th, 2017

NASRINE GROSS

"Imagine how much sustenance that book and so many others could have provided for these people during their darkest hours."

Imagine a country with twenty-five million people. Imagine that one million of their compatriots have died resisting invaders in a series of wars that have lasted twenty-three years. Imagine the land surrounding these people; debris, land mines, chemical poisoning—so much destruction. Now imagine that 90% of the surviving women and 80% of the surviving men cannot read. This is my country; this is Afghanistan, where the very fabric of society has been shredded almost beyond recognition.

Illiteracy in Afghanistan has created human beings that have no idea what is happening outside the confines of their own villages. If these people, my people, cannot read for themselves, how can they possibly differentiate between truth and lies? How can they learn to find clean water, have better hygiene, or identify unexploded shells?

Now imagine if these same people could have read the Koran and distinguished the truths of Islam from doctrine corrupted and twisted into lies preached by the Taliban. Imagine if they could have read the *Shahnameh*, a book like Homer's *Iliad*, which is nearly one thousand years old, one of the world's great classics, and Afghan in origin. Imagine how much sustenance that book and so many others could have provided for these people during their darkest hours.

I was not in Afghanistan during those darkest hours. I was safe in the United States, my adopted country of thirty years. But I never forgot my people, and I was driven by an overwhelming desire to do something to help—something that would make a difference. For years, I had contemplated how Afghanistan and its people could ever achieve peace after so much war and destruction. In 1999, while researching my book, *Steps of Peace and Our Responsibility as Afghans*, a friend referred me to *The Sunflower*, by Simon Wiesenthal.

Although many books have influenced me and led me to my mission in life—my work as an activist for the inalienable rights of women in Afghanistan—*The Sunflower* stands out as having most profoundly touched me and inspired me because it ultimately revolves around the question of closure. Coming to closure is not a simple concept; it is not a one-dimensional activity. It is not like saying, "I am going to have lunch," and then when lunch is finished saying, "It's over—that's it." One cannot just say, "I'm going to forgive," because there are many, many dimensions to forgiveness.

In *The Sunflower*, Mr. Wiesenthal, a Jew imprisoned in a Nazi concentration camp during World War II, recounts being summoned to the bedside of a dying SS soldier, who confesses his heinous crimes, which include murdering children. This soldier asks Wiesenthal to forgive him so that he can die in peace, a request Wiesenthal, who leaves the room without a word, is unable to grant. Thereafter, Wiesenthal is haunted by a fundamental question: Is it possible to forgive without forgetting?

He poses this question to forty-three experts on ethics from around the globe and compiles their responses in his book. It is a phenomenal collection of essays about forgiveness, how people take responsibility for evil actions, and how they assess blame.

The world faces these questions in the wake of 9/11. Should the whole Arab world bear the blame for these crimes? Should a fifteen-year-old Arab boy in a small village be held responsible for these atrocities any more than the children and grandchildren of German citizens during World War II should be held responsible for the heinous crimes committed by the Nazi regime?

I abhor terrorists, who do not even think in human, let alone humane terms. We must help the victims of 9/11 achieve closure to their pain and grief over the injustice they have suffered, without making more innocent people suffer, and without risking new circles of hatred that could lead to future terrorist activity. These are difficult problems faced not only by victims of the tragedies of 9/11 and victims of years of war in Afghanistan, but also by governments and citizens the world over.

War separates people. How can we bring them back together? How can we make them accept that they are different, but that they can live together? What can be forgiven and who can do the forgiving, not just on individual and societal levels, but also on national and international levels?

Sometimes, when pain is very raw, you cannot even think of forgiveness. The Afghan women I meet now who lived under the Taliban tell me about how the Taliban whipped them and beat them through their burkas, over their heads, on their ankles, on their wrists. How can Afghan people find salvation and peace if nobody takes responsibility for the crimes? How can others do justice for these families, bring them to closure, and help them find their way to continue with life?

I believe that if the Afghan people remain in resentment, they remain in the past, in the time the crimes occurred. And I believe that they will not achieve a level of peace unless there is some level of forgiveness. Yet do I, who was safely sheltered in the United States during the atrocities, have any more right to forgive the Taliban on behalf of the Afghan people than Mr. Wiesenthal had the right to forgive a Nazi criminal on behalf of all Jews? I most certainly have even less right than Mr. Wiesenthal and I would not dare say I represent the people of Afghanistan and forgive in their name.

And yet, not having forgiveness is like having a burning coal in the palm of your hand; if you do not throw it away, it only burns you. You remember the perpetrator of the crime, but the perpetrator most often does not remember you. Each person needs to heal herself and himself separately from the criminal, because as long as you have not reached forgiveness, you have not separated yourself from the criminal or the crime.

Afghans need time to heal, whether it is a few months or a few years. They need to have stable jobs. Even though these might be small jobs, Afghans need the reassurance that each day will be the same; each of those days will validate their dignity.

I do not think the people of Afghanistan will ever forget; the tragedies are now woven into their complex societal fabric. But, I do hope and I do believe that Afghans will come to a level of understanding and helping so that they can forgive—so that they too can go on.

Mr. Wiesenthal dedicated his life to preserving the memory of Holocaust victims and fostering tolerance across the globe, trying to ensure that similar tragedies not befall mankind. I am dedicating my life to ensuring that the inalienable rights of women are included in the next constitution of Afghanistan so that the daughters and granddaughters of women who have suffered so much will never again fall victim to crimes perpetrated by groups like the Taliban.

Nasrine Gross

March 11th, 2003

MARIE ELIZABETH HAIST
(QUEEN MIMI)

"I am ninety-one years old as I write this, but I am still young at heart and I can tell you that fairy tales really can come true."

"Fairy tales can come true, it can happen to you, if you're young at heart."
—Frank Sinatra, "Young at Heart"

I am ninety-one years old as I write this, but I am still young at heart and I can tell you that fairy tales really can come true. I know because my own life is a fairy tale—a fairy tale like *Cinderella*.

It might surprise some people who read this to know that I think of my life as a Cinderella story because I had so many hard times. My life didn't play out the way I thought it would when I was a little girl, so many years ago, reading *Cinderella* and dreaming of being a princess.

My father was an immigrant from Romania and he was a fine cabinetmaker. He was also a prince of a man and I loved him dearly. He often talked about the king who walked among commoners, and since Romania had a royal family back then, I thought that my father was that king, secretly walking among common men, which made me a princess—just like Cinderella.

Like many little girls, I dreamed of growing up to marry a handsome prince. I did get married and I had two wonderful daughters, but my husband didn't turn out to be the handsome prince—quite the opposite—and I worked until I was bone weary.

That life came to an end. My marriage ended in divorce. Eventually I lost my house and I lived in a van. Then, I even lost the van. Somehow I found myself living on the streets and I lost touch with my daughters. I was homeless for nine years until one day I wandered into Fox Laundromat on Montana Avenue in Santa Monica.

Stan, the owner, was very kind. He let me sleep in the laundromat one cold, rainy night and I stayed for the next eighteen years. It was still a little scary at times. I would sleep in a chair between the rows of washers, but it was better than sleeping on the streets with no roof over my head.

I helped out at the laundromat and I met so many nice people. I made so many friends and I still do. Some of those people, like Zach Galifianakis and Renée Zellweger, are even movie stars.

People ask me if I was unhappy when I was homeless or when I was living in the laundromat and I always say, "No. Happiness is a choice and I decided a long time ago that my choice was to be happy no matter what. Yesterday is gone. Leave it there."

Maybe that's why I seem to attract so many wonderful people into my life. I know that there are good people and there are bad people, but I meet so many good ones. People are always doing nice things for me, but one day I got a really big surprise. Zach told me he got me an apartment near the laundromat. I couldn't believe it. I just couldn't believe it. After so many years without a home it was like my handsome prince came along when I was eighty-seven and he gave me my very own apartment—my very own little castle. I was shocked and I am eternally grateful.

At the same time I also thought, "Oh my gosh what am I going to do. I don't have any furniture."

Then Renée found out about the apartment and she furnished it for me just like a fairy godmother. She furnished the whole thing. I have a beautiful bed, table, a comfortable chair, and a wonderful TV that Zach bought me. Around this time in my life I also got to know Yaniv, who was a barista at the local coffee shop. We became friends and he started to make a movie about my life.

The movie is called *Queen Mimi* and you can even watch it on Netflix. That's what made me famous. "Famous without pay," as I say. Even though I grew up in Los Angeles surrounded by films my whole life, I never thought that I would be famous. Then all of a sudden there I was, transformed into a princess in my beautiful dress with my hair and my makeup done, stepping into my carriage of a limousine. I went to my very own movie premiere and saw myself on the big screen—like Hollywood royalty.

It is so much fun. I just love every day. People come up to me in the street and they say, "I know you, you're Queen Mimi," or people call the laundromat—where I still go everyday because I love to keep busy, and I love to help people—and they ask to speak to me. After seeing my movie, people have called me from Australia, Germany, Israel, and many more places. My story seems to touch them and that makes me really happy.

So you see, as I said, fairy tales really do come true. Life can be hard on all of us but you have to get back up no matter how bad it seems. If Cinderella had only looked down when she was scrubbing the floors and emptying out the ashes, her life would have never changed. But we must remember that we don't have to look down—looking down is a choice. We can look up. When we look up we see the beautiful blue sky.

I believe that everyone can choose to be happy and grateful by living in the present and by choosing to say what I say every morning and every night: "Thank you, God. Thank you for another day on planet Earth. Thank you, thank you, thank you."

Queen Mimi

January 30th, 2017

SENATOR GARY HART

"Over the years, a lot of my reading has tended toward the confluence of the religious and the spiritual and the social and the political. Writings that have met at those crossroads have always been important to me."

My greatest fear is of being on a desert island with nothing to read. Translate "desert island" to mean dentist's office, doctor's office, airport, or anywhere you have to wait—and there I have to have a book under my arm. I think I've had a book under my arm since I was eight or nine years old.

Where did I get my love of books and reading? I've often thought about that question, but I've never been able to answer it—I suppose it's instinctive. I've been, since my earliest years, a compulsive reader, yet neither of my parents graduated from high school. They encouraged me in school and in every other way and they both read—my mother read the Bible over and over again, until she almost memorized it—but they were not widely literate. And we were, relatively speaking, poor—too poor at least to subscribe to magazines.

When I was in the fourth, fifth, and sixth grades, I used to haunt the Carnegie Public Library in Ottawa, Kansas. Every afternoon, when I wasn't playing sports, I was in that library reading. I was one of those serial, compulsive readers; I'd latch on to an author and read everything that author wrote. I read through all of Zane Gray's novels and all of L. Frank Baum's novels, before eventually migrating to Steinbeck, Joyce, Faulkner, and Hemingway.

My social thinking was heavily influenced by *The Grapes of Wrath*, which I read when I was seventeen or eighteen. Since I grew up among the working people, it resonated with me. *Ulysses*, arguably the greatest novel of the twentieth century, at least in English, and Joyce made a huge impact on me. Joyce also heavily influenced Faulkner, and I've read all of Faulkner. I'm particularly fond of his short story, "The Bear," about Ike McCaslin, a young man who hunts in the Mississippi woods with his relatives every year for a mythical bear; the biggest bear that ever lived. However, no one except for very old men has ever seen the bear. Not until Ike gets lost from the group and finally puts down his rifle, compass, and watch—the symbols of time and place—does he see the bear, the most stunning creature he's ever seen. The bear represents nature and reality; the point being that Ike couldn't see the bear until he got rid of the trappings of civilization. Likewise, Hemingway's *The Old Man and the Sea* is a metaphysical story about the individual seeking truth and finding truth in nature.

From a humanitarian point of view, Victor Hugo's *Les Misérables*, and the social and political impact of the French Revolution influenced my thinking. I also read Tolstoy and was heavily influenced by his epic writing, such as *War and Peace*, but also by his religious writings. Late in life, Tolstoy became very spiritual and broke with the Russian Orthodox Church over the plight of Russia's peasants, because he felt the church cared more about the wealthy and the nobility than about the vast masses of serfs and poor people. One of his last novels, *Resurrection*, is about a man who undergoes a spiritual reformation in his life.

I was raised in a very religious family and I went to a church college. Out of that experience came a social conscience and out of that social conscience came political activism. Over the years, a lot of my reading has tended toward the confluence of the religious and the spiritual and the social and the political. Writings that have met at those crossroads have always been important to me.

I read Kierkegaard when I was in college in the 1950s and again in the seminary in the early 1960s. A particular book of his, *Purity of Heart*, made a great impact on me in terms of the individual's relationship with God and how that is immediate and not through institutions or traditional religious structures.

Thomas Jefferson, whom I've been reading for thirty to forty years, heavily influenced my political thinking. My reading of Jefferson has included not only many books about him, but also his collected works, including the Declaration of Independence and his letters. Jefferson only wrote one book, but he wrote sixty thousand to seventy thousand letters, which contain his political philosophy.

The scope and breadth of Jefferson's thoughts and the compass of his interests was huge. When someone is that interesting you want to know what he was thinking and why he thought it. I continually find interesting and provocative thoughts in his writing. His role as a thirty-three-year-old in the founding of this country and the declaration of its basic principles has seldom been matched in human history. He would be immortalized for the Declaration of Independence alone, but he accomplished so much more. Recently, I wrote my doctoral thesis on Jefferson, so I am imbued with his thinking. One notion of his that people didn't pay much attention to is the importance of war republics and citizen involvement. That could be transposed to the twenty-first century to solve the problem of citizen participation in this country. If I were to put together a library of influences it would certainly include Jefferson's *Selected Letters*.

As I've gotten older, I've tended to go back to the classics. I've read and reread *The Odyssey* and *The Iliad*. All things considered, I would probably put *The Odyssey* at the top of a list of books; it's a timeless tale of man's search for home and struggle to find home, and it's never been exceeded. I think I've read every English translation, because they're all different. However, as someone recently pointed out to me, it took eight hundred years for the story of *The Odyssey* to be put down on paper, so there's a lesson there in patience in terms of writing.

I've written twelve books of my own, including four novels, and I try to deal with my experience through fiction and nonfiction. I am writing my thirteenth book, on grand strategy for the United States in the twenty-first century, so I am currently reading a lot of books on strategy.

I also enjoy light fiction and I've just read *The Company*, by Robert Littell. In fact, I always have a stack of ten or twelve books going at any given time and three or four that I read concurrently—including the light fiction and the spy thrillers, including now Alan Furst—that I enjoy.

Just as I cannot pinpoint exactly why I developed my love of books and reading, I cannot pinpoint a single book that influenced my life, because I have been influenced by a whole library of books. I do know, however, that I cannot imagine life without books, because I couldn't live without them.

June 18th, 2003

"*The Lord of the Rings* was always a meeting place for my father and me when all other means to communicate had left us."

The summer I was five, my father would read me one chapter from *The Hobbit* every evening. Each night, I would beg for two chapters or just a little more. He had a trundle bed and I slept below him and could usually pester him to keep reading. At least that's how I remember it. In truth, I probably passed out most nights in the middle of some monumental action scene, but by the end of August we had finished the book.

I spent the school year with my mom and missed the old man terribly. If I wanted, I could read a few lines from that book and immediately I would hear his voice and feel his arm.

The next summer, we read *The Fellowship of the Ring* and, to this day, I pride myself on being one of the few six-year-olds to march their way through the complexities of the first installment of Tolkien's masterwork. As the metaphors deepened and the characters became more complex and flawed, I'm sure I lost my way, but my love for Bilbo transferred easily to Frodo and I was happy to hear my father's voice again.

The following summer, I deemed myself too cool to be read to, but eventually became a good enough reader to accomplish the trilogy alone. It became a religion to me, a world so much more vibrant than the gray humdrum nature of high school life. Through the awkwardness of teenage years, *The Lord of the Rings* was always a meeting place for my father and me when all other means to communicate had left us.

When my wife was pregnant with our first child, she had a great deal of trouble sleeping, and I began reading her the trilogy at night. Loving the book, she began looking forward to nightfall, simply so she could eat chocolate and listen to the tale unfold. She couldn't have known, but for me sharing that book was when I knew we had become a family. More than the exchange of any wedding vows, some kind of union had occurred over those pages. Even now, I can see my many copies of Tolkien's work sitting on the shelf and they are not books. They are more like threads interwoven in the fabric of my life.

May 1st, 2003

"Holden somehow holds on to some strong corner of my inner being, more than a half century after I first met him."

Certain works of art get you, at certain times in your life, in ways that are so strong and powerful that they last you a lifetime. The number of young people—for over a half century now—who were profoundly moved at an early age by *The Catcher in the Rye*, testifies to the lasting strength of J. D. Salinger's unique yet universal voice and his power to capture the emotions of generation after generation of the eternal adolescent in all of us, seemingly defying all differences in time and space.

For me like so many others at the time, it was in the mid-1950s, as I came of age, that I first read it. When I made my first film in 1970, *A Safe Place*, it was still haunting me. Though I had written that film, like the play it is based on, with a female protagonist—played by Karen Black in the play, Tuesday Weld in the movie—I only realized several years later that I was actually writing it about myself, still deeply haunted by Holden Caulfield in an inexplicable yet undeniable way.

And even now, strange as it is to admit it, Holden somehow holds on to some strong corner of my inner being, more than a half century after I first met him. He never entirely goes away.

What is the power and magic of Salinger's book that for so many, like myself, seems to transcend time? What does it have in common with the novels of Philip Roth or the plays of Arthur Miller that similarly rocked my being much more recently? Or, for that matter, with Proust's Madeleine and Anaïs Nin's *Diaries*, T. S. Eliot's "The Wasteland" and, God knows, Shakespeare's sonnets? What is it that is so vividly captured about life in a certain written work that it can reach deep into one's brain and one's heart with such a strong grip that it holds on to you for a lifetime?

Who knows. But that is what *The Catcher in the Rye* was the very first work of art to do for me and that is the true wonder of art, the magic to be found—most especially inside the covers of a book—the great and deeply lasting gift that writers have given us down through the centuries. Sure, they may entertain you and excite you and enrich your life, but *well* beyond that, they can actually *change* it, profoundly, in so many astonishing ways.

But I'm getting too heavy, as my generation used to put it. You know what I'm trying to say, don't you? Read a book and see for yourself. Any book if you really want to know, Holden. Because the world is *truly* just a book away, as the man said!

December 14th, 2016

SENATOR EDWARD M. KENNEDY

"I reread the final sentences of his book and I am reminded of him and his challenge to strive for the quality he admired most—courage."

There are many books that have influenced me over the years, which I have found to be both illuminating and memorable. However, if I have to pick the one book that continues to have the most meaning for me, it would be President Kennedy's *Profiles in Courage.*

This Pulitzer Prize-winning book is about remarkable episodes in the lives of eight historic men of principle who, while serving in public office, made very difficult and courageous decisions. These decisions were often made at risk to their office and even their livelihood. In some cases, they lost everything but their honor. The stories of John Quincy Adams, Daniel Webster, Sam Houston, Thomas Hart Benton, Edmund G. Ross, Lucius Quintus Cincinnatus Lamar II, George Norris, and Robert Taft provide continuing inspiration to all who serve in public office or aspire to do so. They are a reminder of the meaning of honorable service and the courage that it often takes.

Even though *Profiles in Courage* was originally published back in 1956, it remains uniquely timeless. Each generation of new young leaders has found it to be an invaluable guide for how to honorably represent their constituents and their country. It is also the book, which those who have been elected and fortunate enough to serve many years still seek out. We reread it when difficult decisions lie ahead of us. For in its dog-eared pages we continue to find inspiration and lessons for today.

The focus of chapter six, Senator Edmund G. Ross of Kansas, is one of the most memorable stories. He turned out to be the deciding vote on whether to impeach President Andrew Johnson. He stood up to unimaginable pressure and was denounced and vilified when he voted not guilty. What had once been a promising career was ruined. As he said to his wife after the impeachment trial, "Millions of men cursing me today will bless me tomorrow for having saved the country from the greatest peril through which it has ever passed, though none but God can ever know the struggle it has cost me."

In time it was finally understood, as stated in Kansas newspapers just before Senator Ross died, that his vote turned the tide against legislative mob rule and "the country was saved from calamity greater than war, while it consigned him to a political martyrdom, the most cruel in our history." From Edmund G. Ross, we learn anew the lesson of political courage, and because of his courage and his character, he is remembered as a shining example of those qualities to this very day.

My brother would be interested to know that his book has inspired the Profile in Courage Award—given each year in his memory to an elected official from the local, state, or national level who has stood up for principle under great pressure and at great risk. Those honored with the award have had their achievements written about and documented as part of a sequel called *Profiles in Courage for Our*

Time, edited by his beloved daughter Caroline. It proves to us that political courage was not just a thing of the past, and we can be very proud of that fact. Jack's book and the vital message it instills has a living legacy, and I know he would be especially pleased by that fact.

Each time I pick up my copy of *Profiles in Courage*, I think of my brother and the lessons he taught me. Not a day goes by that I don't think of him and miss him. I reread the final sentences of his book and I am reminded of him and his challenge to strive for the quality he admired most—courage.

For as he wrote many years ago, "These stories of past courage can define that ingredient—they can teach, they can offer hope, they can provide inspiration. But they cannot supply courage itself. For this, each man must look into his own soul."

November 24th, 2003

TAOISEACH ENDA KENNY

"And so his role in the creation of the very fabric of modern Ireland is very clear."

Though I have read and been inspired by many wonderful books in my lifetime, one which I read relatively recently really struck a chord with me in terms of the sheer strength of character of its subject. Timothy Egan's *The Immortal Irishman: The Irish Revolutionary Who Became an American Hero* recounts the terribly short but incredibly influential life of Irish nationalist Thomas Francis Meagher. His story spans oceans and continents, and his presence in the hearts of the Irish, I believe, is eternal.

Meagher's position in nineteenth century Irish society was one of great privilege. His father was a wealthy businessman, a former mayor, and, even more significantly, a member of the British parliament, making him one of a tiny minority of Irish Catholic families with assets and status. Of course, this conflict within his family made his eventual rebellion at England's oppression of his native land—and its response to a famine in which one million people perished—all the more unique and significant.

As a consequence of his upbringing, Meagher benefited from an excellent education, some of it in England, during which he made a great stir, winning various awards for poetry and debating. His gift for eloquence would remain a part of his character until the end.

He went on to join the radical Young Ireland movement, his rousing, passionate speeches earning him the nickname "Meagher of the Sword" and the attention of forces who sought to quash the movement for which he was becoming an important figure. It was during his time as a Young Irelander that Meagher visited France, hoping to find inspiration and rally support for his nationalist cause.

Although neither material nor political support of significance came of his expedition, he did find inspiration for what became the enduring symbol of his beloved Ireland—the Irish tricolor flag of green, white, and gold. And so his role in the creation of the very fabric of modern Ireland is very clear.

Escaping from a sentence that would have had him live out his years in "Van Diemen's Land"—Tasmania as we know it today—Meagher fled to New York, where he continued to advocate for Irish nationalism. Even so, he became involved in United States politics, eventually becoming governor of the Territory of Montana decades before it became the forty-first state in 1889.

In 1867, at the age of 44, Meagher's brief life ended when he drowned in the Missouri River near Fort Benton, Montana. A revolutionary, a patriot, a soldier, and a politician—Meagher led a life of bravery and passion, and he was always possessed of a relentless desire to pursue the betterment of the country he loved for the people he championed his entire life.

The wonderful book by Timothy Egan quotes one of Meagher's verses—yes, he was a poet, too—that beautifully captures the remarkable longevity of his passion:

> I would not die! I would not die!
> In Youth's bright hour of pleasure;
> I would not leave without a sigh,
> The dreams, the hopes, I treasure.

That excerpt also conveys something of a melancholy tone that is truly an important part of his story, given how early he was lost to the world. Thomas Francis Meagher was a true son of Ireland, and I would certainly encourage everyone to read this amazing story of his dreams and hopes.

Enda Kenny

December 20th, 2016

IRVIN KERSHNER

"I have never lost the thrill of escaping into a new book and thereby embarking upon a new adventure."

What books have influenced me over the years? There have been too many to count: French, Italian, English, American, and other authors as well. At one time, I wanted to be a writer, but I realized I didn't have the particular drive one needs. But, the act of reading continued to give my life greater meaning. I fell in love with many authors, ranging from Flaubert to Tolstoy, Zola to Poe, and Twain to Vonnegut, whom I consider one of the most misunderstood and underappreciated writers of our time.

Early in life, I learned that through reading and particularly through reading great books, we gain a much better understanding of human nature. If you want to understand Napoleon, for example, read *War and Peace*. If you want to understand the charm and self-righteous purity of Americans, read Mark Twain.

Just as reading provides insight, not reading and being deprived of books is painful for anyone who understands their true value. I first fully understood the importance of books when they weren't readily available at the air force base where I was stationed outside of London during World War II. Being in Europe during the war was adventure enough, but I hungered for books and I remember the day that the first box of paperbacks arrived. Paperback books were a new phenomenon and suddenly we had piles of them, the classics, poetry, philosophy, history, all printed on inexpensive newsprint. For me, and for some men in my bomber squadron, those books were more than a welcome escape; they were sustenance.

My experience during the war helped me better understand and appreciate the luxury of having books available. And although it is difficult for me to pinpoint any one book that most influenced me through the years, I have never lost the thrill of escaping into a new book and thereby embarking upon a new adventure.

I read *Out of My Later Years* about ten years ago. In this book, Einstein questions many of the beliefs that constitute the so-called wisdom of the ages. The book reinforced my own belief that you mustn't take anything at face value and that you must question everything.

According to Einstein, "common sense" is the accumulated prejudices of a person up to about the age of eighteen. He wrote that "imagination is more important than knowledge." This idea resonated with me. I have often visualized the many thousands or even millions of times through the ages children walked along the shore with their parents or with teachers who warned them never to go beyond the line they saw at the end of the horizon because the earth was flat and they would fall off. After all, it looked flat and the concept of the earth as a big flat table seemed to be common sense.

Out of My Later Years helped to clarify many of my own thoughts on life and the world we live in. I have tried to read some of Einstein's other books, but his mind was so complex. I lose my way. *Out of My Later Years* provides us with unique insight into that complex mind of his and an understanding of how one of the most brilliant men who ever lived viewed the world around him. Reading can expand our horizons beyond what we accept as common sense.

September 7th, 2007

RIZ KHAN

"In many ways, I have spent my life caught between cultures."

For me, reading is absolutely essential. It is an opportunity to live, travel, and see the world through other people's eyes and other people's experiences. This is why it is so important to read a diverse range of topics.

In many ways, I have spent my life caught between cultures. I was born in the British colony of Aden, which later became part of the communist People's Democratic Republic of Yemen. I grew up in what was a very wealthy family that lost pretty much everything in the scramble to get out during the violence and conflict in 1966. I was only four. That journey took us to London, where, after my mother and father divorced, my mother struggled to bring up my younger brother and me on a very minimal wage; at that time, equivalent to about $10 a week, and we all lived in one room. Even though we had a financially tough time, my mother managed to make us feel like we had everything other children had and focused on making sure we studied hard. Part of that was to encourage us to read, and I did!

I read almost everything I could get my hands on, and spent a lot of time in the local library, where I loved the choice of books and the wonderfully calm atmosphere. Apart from the education, and sense of escape the stories gave me, visiting the library was a very economical way for us to have something very rich and diverse easily at hand. It didn't cost anything to go to the library and read, and it was an exciting opening of so many doors and ideas. I believe that this kind of access to stories and information is incredibly valuable in broadening one's perspective on the world. It was certainly true for me. In the library, I would pick up and read almost anything, from comics, which had a deep impact on me because I found I was a natural artist and cartoonist (I still draw cartoons from time to time), to fantasy fiction like *The Lord of the Rings* and *The Hobbit*, later moving on to books I considered great fiction, such as *The World According to Garp*, by the incredibly talented American author John Irving.

Experience with books and the joy they brought was a part of my life from my earliest years. This continued through university, and very much into my career as a journalist, where I have to read a lot every day to stay on top of news and current affairs. I wish I had more time to read fiction nowadays, but my job takes up a lot of my time.

In the late 1980s and early 1990s, on my long commutes to work through the terrible traffic of London's rush hour, I would often listen to shows on BBC Radio that featured book reviews and interviews with authors. When I heard about a book that sounded interesting, I would often go out and buy it. One of these books was *The Remains of the Day*, by Japanese-British author Kazuo Ishiguro, which won the Man Booker Prize for fiction in 1989 and was later adapted into an Academy Award-nominated film.

It is a very emotional and a very moving book. At first, what struck me most was that an author of Japanese origin could have such an insightful understanding of British character, particularly the stiff upper lip behavior in the lead-up to World War II. This rigidity of the British of that era is portrayed through flashbacks in the life of the main character, Stevens, a butler to a wealthy American man, Mr. Farraday. As the story unfolds, the reader learns that Stevens's former employer, Lord Darlington, advocated negotiations with Hitler, which troubled the butler, although he felt it was never his position to make any comment to his master. In his interactions with Darlington and Farraday, Stevens's behavior is governed by loyalty to his employer. With his loyalty, he sacrifices his personal life in a way that would almost be unfathomable to the youth of today, including his unspoken, but deep feelings for the head housekeeper, Miss Kenton. In many ways Stevens himself was caught between two cultures, as the world of master and servant he had been groomed for evaporated in post-World War II Britain.

Growing up in Britain in the late 1960s and 1970s, I experienced the residual elements of Victorian and post-Victorian culture in Britain as Stevens lived it, a culture based around rules and rigidity. This was perhaps most evident in my time as a cadet in the Air Training Corps (ATC), an adventure club essentially run by the British Royal Air Force, where old traditions are kept intact. I identified with Stevens's character in part because of his internal conflict, the feeling of being torn between two systems, and in part because I experienced the last vestiges of his world with some of the older British people I got to meet and know.

The Great Britain of my youth was rapidly changing from the polite, stratified, and even rigid culture, so beautifully described in *The Remains of the Day*. There were still strong elements of it that I could witness in some of my elderly teachers, and those I met through the ATC. Those were times when students would stand up and straighten their ties before leaving or entering a classroom, running an errand, or speaking to a teacher. Those aspects of British character still resonate with me.

I have also lived through the transition in British society, which has been both good and bad. Today, Britain is a much more mixed society with tremendous cultural and ethnic diversity. At the same time, however, it has lost much of the politeness and discipline of the past, and that can be seen in the way people interact with each other. There is far more aggression and violence, also a greater sense of competitiveness that is often counterproductive to good and cooperative social behavior. Crime, particularly violent crime, has increased.

Although I was not looking for the book, *The Remains of the Day*, to help me better understand my character, I did feel connected with elements of Britain's history and character, which helped shape the world around me. It stirred me emotionally, both as a story and as a testament to a dying era.

As with the books of my earliest childhood, it allowed me to travel through time and experience the world through someone else's eyes, and moved me because it carried echoes of my own personal experience with British character.

June 6th, 2009

AMBASSADOR JEANE J. KIRKPATRICK

"By the time I was six, reading was my principle activity."

My mother often said that I was a self-taught reader by the age of four. Reading was my favorite pastime as a child and books were always my favorite Christmas presents. By the time I was six, reading was my principle activity. I read everything from *The Bobbsey Twins* and *Nancy Drew*, to *The Hardy Boys*. I never really worried about girls' books and boys' books; they were all wonderful stories and I enjoyed them tremendously.

Since I have been such a book person and such an avid reader from a very early age, I find it entirely impossible to identify a single book that has touched my life in the most significant way. Scores of books from a wide variety of authors have touched me in many different ways at different stages in my life and continue to do so.

Particular books and particular authors began to play major roles in my life in junior high school. I was greatly impressed by *The Swiss Family Robinson*, for example. Although their adventures didn't appeal to me as I got older, they struck me as absolutely wonderful at the time. At that age, I also found Kipling's stories—*The Jungle Book*, *Kim*, and others—very exciting and moving.

When I was in the seventh grade, my family moved from Duncan, Oklahoma, where I was born, to Vandalia, Illinois. At the time, I was very interested in the Civil War, Abraham Lincoln, Robert E. Lee, and the abolitionists who had settled not far from our new hometown. Because of my family's migration from the South to the North, I read about the Civil War first from a Southern perspective and then from a Northern perspective. This taught me a valuable lesson early in life: The person who writes history has an impact on the history that gets written. Its study is called the sociology of knowledge, and it's a discipline that has interested me ever since.

In Vandalia, I spent a great deal of time at our public library and more or less stumbled into major literature including Alexandre Dumas's *The Count of Monte Cristo*; Victor Hugo's *Les Misérables*; and Charles Dickens's *David Copperfield* and *Oliver Twist*. I also stumbled into American literature, including the works of Nathaniel Hawthorne and Washington Irving. It was a wonderful period of adventure, lived through the pages of great works.

Shakespeare first came to my attention in high school. *Julius Caesar* was the first Shakespearean play that excited me, and it launched me into a lifelong passion for his work. I'm sure I did not fully comprehend his plays at the time, but I was deeply engrossed as I read them, and I return to tragedies and histories again and again.

My interest in female authors blossomed as I completed high school and matriculated at Columbia. I read George Eliot in those years, whom I liked a great deal and by whom I was very moved. I read all of Jane Austen and Virginia Woolf, whose novels I devoured and whose essay, "A Room of One's Own," remains my favorite feminist classic. But my enthusiasm was not limited to women writers. Those were also the years I devoured D. H. Lawrence's novels and poems.

French literature became increasingly important to me in college and French literature ultimately attracted me to France. In graduate school, I was awarded a French government fellowship and I spent a year and a half studying there. That influenced my professional development, but France had a much greater impact on me than that. France was the first country I visited outside of the United States. I fell in love with France and I've been in love with it ever since.

Balzac's *Le père Goriot*, Flaubert's *Madame Bovary*, and many other French novels are dramatic tales with very powerful depictions of character. Balzac and Flaubert are among the authors whose complete works I have in my library—I have read and reread them throughout my life. I was also much taken by Camus—his novels, such as *The Stranger*, *The Plague*, and *The First Man*, and his essays, especially *The Rebel*. I was in France at the time of the great debates between Camus and Sartre about revolution and Communism. I found Camus a much more sensible man than Sartre and I still do. Like George Orwell, Camus rejected the Marxist promise of revolutionary utopianism and focused on reality. Although I also read Sartre, I found his political understanding inadequate.

Russian writers from Dostoyevsky, to Tolstoy, Pushkin, Pasternak, Solzhenitsyn, and Nabokov have also had a major impact on me. Communism is a dreadful political system that destroyed freedom for millions of people around the world. However, even during the depths of Communism in Russia, I always felt that anyone who believed Russia was not a Western country had never read Russian literature. I think the experience of Russian literature left me with a lesser tendency to oversimplify, or exaggerate. I have found Nabokov especially intriguing. His small volume *Bend Sinister* is the most compelling and insightful treatment of totalitarian dictatorships I have ever read—and I have read a good deal on this subject. *Pale Fire* was and is a special treat for me.

Many of the books I have mentioned have influenced the way I view politics and life. Although I find it impossible to identify a single book that has touched my life in the most significant way, the unifying thread that weaves its way through the wonderful books and authors that have enriched my life is the thread of reality. The authors I most admire and find myself rereading through the years have written books that reject a utopian view of life, society, and politics. They tend to see the world from a perspective that is both more complex and realistic.

The contemporary American works I have most enjoyed and learned from are, I think, those of Saul Bellow and Vladimir Nabokov (or is he only Russian?). I have greatly enjoyed Bellow's novels, including *The Dean's December* and the controversial *Ravelstein*. Somewhat to my surprise, I was also much impressed by Philip Roth's *American Pastoral*.

If I were required on pain of death to identify the single book that has had the greatest influence on my intellectual life, I would name Plato's *Republic*, from which I have taught many students. His analysis of the relations among character, culture, constitution, and change is brilliant and endlessly illuminating. I have learned much more than I have taught from Plato.

I have been and remain a person who lives in significant measure through books. I cannot conceive of life without literature but fortunately, I do not need to. One of the many pleasures of parenthood was reading to my three sons when they were young, and introducing them to the pleasures of good books.

Jeane J Kirkpatrick

November 13th, 2003

JUDE LAW

"I read it at an age when children become adolescents, who want to become adults, and I distinctly remember feeling that I could start reading the books my parents read."

Books provide unique emotional inlets and outlets in my life, roles they have played for as long as I can remember. When I feel emotionally overwhelmed, drained, or at a loss of motivation, I can always retreat into a book. I can always escape into a story.

Of the many books that have influenced my life, two mark important transitions—one from the realm of boys to the world of men, the other from the realm of men to the world of proud fathers.

Animal Farm entered my life through the theatrical version, which I saw performed at the National Theatre when I was twelve. I was so taken with the production that my mother bought me a copy of the book. Although other books had played a rich part in my life prior to *Animal Farm*, Orwell's novel marked the first time I recall reading a book that spoke to me on many levels, as if I were leaving the world of straightforward storytelling intended for children and entering the more multilayered world of adult books. I read it at an age when children become adolescents, who want to become adults, and I distinctly remember feeling that I could start reading the books my parents read, instead of books specifically written for children.

In *Animal Farm*, Orwell led me into a world that, on one level, is about as far removed from the human world as possible. At the same time, I was immediately emotionally engaged and affected by the manipulation and dominance of Napoleon, the pig; the frailty and death of Boxer, the horse; and the demise of the innocent farm animals as a whole. *Animal Farm* captured my attention because it was an engaging read, but it affected me because I was aware of the underlying commentary woven through the story and seen through the eyes of these animals.

The Hobbit marks a different and more recent transition in my life. I didn't read the book when I was younger. In fact, I first read it two years ago, when I read it to my son, Raff. I have always read to my children, but *The Hobbit* was the first book Raff and I read together that didn't have a lot of pictures in it. It was quite a dark, complicated, and adult world for him, but he adored it. He was five at the time, and reading that book together was the beginning of a new stage in our relationship. Rather than sharing a book through pictures on the page, we shared the story through the world of imagination inside his head.

Imagination comes out in children through their play, through their drawing—through just about everything. But there is a stillness that is rare with little children, especially little boys. I saw that stillness in Raff each time we read *The Hobbit*. It was obvious that he realized the freedom that reading afforded him, as he just lay back and let the words drift into the room. This was a big step for him; retreating inside his head, inside his imagination on a very personal level, and it's a step that he has now absolutely embraced.

Perhaps I'm biased, because of my work with the arts, but I feel that helping to instill in my children the same love of reading that has so enriched my life is one of my most important roles as a father. It is a role I take very seriously and it is a role that enriches my own life beyond measure.

October 22nd, 2003

NORMAN LEAR

"My life without books would be like my life without clothes—naked."

Given my chosen profession, it is perhaps surprising that I was not a big reader in my youth. My parents never read to me and reading didn't really play an important role in my life until I was in my mid-teens. Today, I read day-to-day, topical publications, almost with a sense of addiction. I read three or four newspapers in the morning, and I read many of the weekly magazines; my house is sinking under the weight of magazines.

Of course, I also read books. I enjoy biographies and I just finished *Bush at War*, by Bob Woodward and *John Adams*, by David McCullough. I also enjoy essays, and I am currently reading *How to Be Alone: Essays*, by Jonathan Franzen.

Now that I'm eighty, as I reflect on all that I've read, one book stands above the crowd: *Emerson's Essays*. Nothing has touched me more or moved me more than this volume of his work. I read it first when I was sixteen or seventeen. Since that time, Emerson has been my Gideon. I still have the same worn copy. I always enjoy flipping through the pages and rereading passages I underlined more than sixty years ago. I often carry it in my briefcase, I often bring it on trips, and it sits beside me now as I write:

> To believe your own thoughts, to believe what is true for you in your private heart is true for all men; that is genius . . . A man should learn to detect and watch that gleam of light, which flashes across his mind from within, more than the luster of the firmament of bards and sages. Yet he dismisses without notice his thought, because it is his. In every work of genius, we recognize our own rejected thoughts. They come back to us with a certain alienated majesty. Great works of art have no more affecting lesson for us than that. They teach us to abide by our spontaneous impressions with good-humored inflexibility more than when the whole cry of voices is on the other side. Else tomorrow a stranger will say, with masterly good sense, precisely what we have thought and felt all the time. And we shall be forced to take with shame our own opinion from another.

I can't express how much I love that passage. I have read the same thought—finding one's own truth and following one's own path—worded in so many ways by so many different people, but Emerson's eloquence has stuck with me.

I have found the greatest joy in exercising my own vital ability—synthesizing the essence of a complicated thought or group of thoughts and mainlining it to a large audience—in a life for which I am terribly grateful.

There have been moments of doubt; many moments of doubt. Early in my career, I had a week to write a very short monologue for Tennessee Ernie Ford. At 2:00 a.m. on the day before it was due, I still hadn't written a word for the 10:00 a.m. table reading.

How many times have I carried on and cried, believing I would never write another word—and then, under the pressure of the clock, suddenly coughed it up? I can't say that I remember thinking per se of words from *Emerson's Essays* during those difficult times, but I have no doubt that I derived inspiration from them. In those words, I found quintessential truth.

There are 360 degrees of routes in life to each and every truth. You travel most of them before the truth you seek locks in and you own it. And so I continue to look for kernels of truth in my much-loved and well-worn copy of *Emerson's Essays*, and indeed I continue to find them.

My life without books would be like my life without clothes—naked. Like everyone else, I know that books warm up a room, but they do much more than that. They warm up the soul.

March 22nd, 2003

LISA LING

"It challenges readers to push their boundaries and take risks;
to not be satisfied with being ordinary—to be extraordinary."

Introducing kids to reading early on sets them up for unlimited adventures and experiences for the rest of their lives. Despite how inundated we are with media, books let us inhabit worlds and remember them in ways that no other media allows.

I would have to say that the book that inspired me most in my life is *Oh, the Places You'll Go!* by Dr. Seuss. As children, we are most impressionable. I vividly remember the world this book opened for me.

It was part of a group of books given to me as a birthday gift from my Aunt Anna and Uncle Jack. I must have been in kindergarten when I first read it, because I actually recall taking this particular book to school with me to show my teacher, Mrs. Clay.

Oh, the Places You'll Go! is about possibilities. It challenges readers to push their boundaries and take risks; to not be satisfied with being ordinary—to be extraordinary. It also encourages people not to get down on themselves if things don't go the way they hoped; because these things will inevitably happen in life.

It made me want to explore and try things about which I'd always been curious. It made me want to stand out and pursue my dreams. This really speaks to just how important a role a single book can play in the life of a child or an adult.

Now I am experiencing *Oh, the Places You'll Go!* all over again, through the eyes of a mother reading to my toddler. As I delight at the wonder in her eyes, it harkens back to the thoughts that I had when I was a kid and excites me all over again—with childlike wonder—about what the world has to offer.

December 6th, 2016

YO-YO MA

"In an effort to be more like him, I began to look at my world through detective eyes."

I must have been about six years old when I found Antoine de Saint-Exupéry's *The Little Prince* on the bookshelf at my family's home in Paris. I was just beginning to experience the joy of books and I found myself immediately captivated at the first page by the fabulous line drawing of "a boa constrictor digesting an elephant." Reading that book was like stepping from my little world into a fantastic journey filled with asteroids, baobab trees, and royalty in ermine robes. *The Little Prince* and I became fast friends.

When my family moved to the United States, the books that had been the source of such joy to me took on new meaning, helping to ease the transition from the culture of my homeland to our new surroundings. I found *The Little Prince* again, this time in English, and it helped me learn the language of my new country.

The love of adventure that was so appealing, I discovered again at the age of eight or nine in *The Adventures of Sherlock Holmes* by Sir Arthur Conan Doyle. Sherlock Holmes was an intriguing character who used intelligence and wit to solve incredibly complex mysteries, often with only the most minute of clues. Each chapter drew me into a distant world of intrigue. How could a child resist reading with exotic titles like *A Scandal in Bohemia*? As the adventures unfolded, Holmes became a real hero to me. The fact that he was an amateur violinist made for an even stronger bond! In an effort to be more like him, I began to look at my world through detective eyes. I felt sure that the methods of deduction Holmes used to solve his clients' dilemmas could be applied to all aspects of life. Even in music, I searched for the clues that would help me better understand and convey a composer's thoughts.

As a youngster, my favorite books were touchstones, but as I grew older, I appreciated them from a new perspective. I look back at *The Little Prince* and see life's lessons. I see Holmes now as a deeply faceted character and recognize the parallel that formed so many years ago between his detective methods and my musical education. Reading continues to spark my sense of curiosity. It has helped me to understand the richness of our cultural differences as well as our common bonds, and has provided me the language to convey a composer's musical story across many cultures. The world is, truly, just a book away.

October 29th, 2004

WILMA MANKILLER

"The book, by telling the individual story of a family in a community, and placing it in a historical and community context, made everything crystal clear to me."

I grew up on my grandfather's Cherokee allotment, Mankiller Flats, near Stilwell, Oklahoma, within the historic boundaries of the Cherokee Nation. We had no indoor plumbing, no electricity, and no paved roads near our house, but we did have books. My father loved to read. As a child, he was sent to Sequoyah Boarding School, a government boarding school. My father spent eleven years at Sequoyah School and had some negative experiences, but one of the positive things that emerged from that experience was a love of reading.

As a result, books always played an important part in my life. As a large, poor family with eleven children, what we loved most were books and board games. There were always books around the house and, in many ways, those books connected us to the outside world. Everyone in my family is an avid reader and, to this day, although I have access to all the modern conveniences, I still can't think of anything better than having the time to sit down with a cup of coffee or tea and read a good book.

My love of books has taken me in many different directions across the years. I love Native American literature, storytelling, scholarly work, and poetry, for example. Vine Deloria, Jr.'s, *God is Red* is my all-time favorite book by a Native American author. He takes very complicated issues of Native American spirituality, culture, and lifeways and makes them all comprehensible to people with little knowledge about Native Americans.

As an adult, I can clearly identify two books that had a profound effect on my life and on my work: Paulo Freire's *Pedagogy of the Oppressed* and Chinua Achebe's *Things Fall Apart*. *Pedagogy of the Oppressed* describes a Brazilian priest's work with Brazilian landless farmers, teaching them to read and write. In the process, he also teaches them a great deal about land ownership, and their rights as human beings.

In reading that book, I learned that poor people and oppressed people sometimes internalize their oppressor. They have to reach a point from which they can be liberated from that internalized oppressor before they can move forward. Freire's book is really just a simple story of a Brazilian priest and his literacy project, but the way he describes his work, his unique understanding of the dynamics of poverty, and the way he used his knowledge to enable people to become strong advocates for themselves had a profound impact on me.

After reading *Pedagogy of the Oppressed* for the first time, as a Native American living and working in often troubled communities, I began to understand the degree to which external historical factors had an impact on my being in the situation I was in, on my family being in the situation it was in, on my community being in the situation it was in, and on my people being in the situation they were in.

Understanding this was liberating, because I came to realize that it wasn't our fault as Cherokee people, any more than it was the fault of those landless Brazilian farmers. It was, however, up to us to figure out how to move forward. I was in my late twenties when I read *Pedagogy of the Oppressed* and I had already been working on Native American issues for quite some time. After reading it, I began to apply some of the principles and values I learned to my work for the next twenty-five years. Those principles and values all turned out to be absolutely correct. I started working on specific rural projects, through which an entire community would come together, decide upon their common goal, and move forward to achieve that goal. In fact, *Pedagogy of the Oppressed* had such a profound impact on me that I traveled to upstate New York to hear Paulo Freire when he lectured at Cornell University as a very elderly man. I had the opportunity to meet him, which I will never forget.

Things Fall Apart describes the disintegration of an African family and community as a result of outside forces. Their traditional system of government is dismantled and supplanted by a colonial government. Their medicine men are ridiculed; their children are taken and put in schools distant from the community. It isn't a political story, in that it doesn't describe the political system behind the disintegration. It is simply the story of one family and one community—what happens to them and how things indeed fall apart.

Reading *Things Fall Apart* broadened my view and helped me to understand the similarity between the Native American experience in this country and what happened to colonized people the world over, and most particularly in South Africa, where the story is set. When I read the book in the early 1970s there was a lot of talk about apartheid and South Africa, but the news reported a dizzying array of political organizations, what they were doing, and who was doing what to whom, without the historical context for what was happening. The book, by telling the individual story of a family in a community, and placing it in a historical and community context, made everything crystal clear to me.

For the past nine years, I've served on the board of the Ford Foundation, which conducts a significant amount of work in South Africa. I believe that *Things Fall Apart* has helped me gain a better understanding of the most important work we can undertake in those communities.

Pedagogy of the Oppressed and *Things Fall Apart* talk about human beings who lived within a community and were part of an extended kinship system in which all the people had some sort of reciprocal relationship. I could relate to and understand that because community is important to Cherokee people. In historic times, there was a tremendous sense of community for the Cherokee people. There were specific ceremonies that were designed to undergird common values among people and to affirm and strengthen the sense of community.

I lived in California for almost twenty years, but in 1976, returned to live in our rural Oklahoma Cherokee community. Even today after everything that has happened to our people, I can still see a very, very strong sense of community among rural Cherokee, which gives me hope.

August 23rd, 2003

JUAN N. SILVA MEZA

"The novel offers us a great constitutional lesson."

One of the books that most influenced my love for reading was the novel *Los de Abajo*, written by Mariano Azuela and published in 1916.

The work showed me, for the first time, literature's power to reproduce not only voices, tones, and figures of speech, but also contexts and dramaturgic tonalities, and to offer explanations of social reality.

Los de Abajo is not only a purely realistic novel. Of course, its re-creation of battles, passages, places, and situations is not symbolic. Nonetheless, the text allows taking a glimpse of the exploration of the trauma that the revolution, with all its horrors, excesses, and mistakes, caused in the national collective consciousness. The exploration of this topic also characterizes later novels, which are undoubtedly Mexican classics, and were inspired by *Los de Abajo* and delve into the psychological study of the 1910 armed conflict.

Additionally, this novel allowed me to get to know and enjoy a language that is almost lost now: the language of the woman soldier that materialized in the Mexican Revolution and that carried—figuratively—Mexico's cultural and linguistic tradition as a link between the twentieth century and the colonial era. In this book, I could also appreciate, for the first time, the literary effect of the change in oral registry, which is necessary to read postrevolution Mexican literature.

In *Los de Abajo*, due to Azuela's stylistic depuration, one can find reminiscences of the picaresque novel, *El Periquillo Sarniento*—published exactly one hundred years before—and the trails of several anthropological paragraphs of later Mexican novels, like *La Muerte de Artemio Cruz* or *El Rey Viejo*.

Mariano Azuela's novel also taught me that the narrative construction of literary characters, which belittles the historically constructed characters, is possible in literature. As a reader of *Los de Abajo*, one cannot argue that the rise and fall of Demetrio Macías overshadows Villa's or Carranza's misfortunes. Also the abuses and excesses of characters like Margarito, Pintada, Pancracio, or Manteca, distract the reader's attention from Huerta's state treason.

Los de Abajo illustrated my understanding of the world as a law professional and constitutional judge. The novel's emotional effect is immediate and cannot be missed by its readers: In face of the decadence and destruction generated by an inevitable armed conflict, one has to be grateful that Mexico is, since 1917, a country governed by a constitutional regime—always improvable, of course—but since then, uninterrupted.

The novel offers us a great constitutional lesson, even after almost one hundred years of publication, namely: In Mexico, nobody that has known desolation, hunger, insecurity, and war, can rationally bet on abandoning the path of peace and justice, institutions and laws that the constitution—product of this war—allowed us to build.

January 8th, 2014

JENNY J. MING

"I believe that books travel with us through life."

I believe that books travel with us through life. I am a passionate reader and many books have made the journey through life with me, gracing the shelves of the various apartments and houses I have called home.

When I first read a book, I generally find that I only understand the aspects that relate to my life up to that point. Of course, as I get older and have more life experience, I can relate to more aspects of the books I read. I also find that each time I reread a book that has moved me, new elements unfold. And although I have returned to many of my favorite books through the years, one stands apart from the others as signposting the cultural lessons I have learned as I have aged.

This particular book would have never come to my attention if my family had stayed in our native city, the former Portuguese colony of Macau. However, my parents decided to immigrate to the United States to provide their five children with better opportunities in life than they themselves had been afforded. And so, at the age of nine, unable to speak a single word of English, I found myself living in the strange and exotic city of San Francisco.

I knew that I had to go back to school eventually, but I will never forget the fear I felt when that day arrived. My mother walked me to the enormous brick building, Spring Valley School, and turned me over to a tall man who stood in front of a room filled with boys and girls in the fourth grade, most of whom were Caucasian and most of whom seemed to be staring past me. My mother then told me that this man was the teacher and that I was to behave, which didn't seem difficult, since he looked much friendlier than the teachers I had had in Macau.

Much to my relief the teacher, who clearly wanted to make me feel comfortable, led me to an empty desk beside a little Chinese girl. I greeted her politely in Cantonese, my native language, and she replied in what I would later learn was a different dialect of Chinese. She might as well have been speaking English like the other children, because I couldn't understand a word she said. So I just settled in and did what seemed natural; I imitated everything she did. She placed her paper in front of her and I placed my paper in front of me. She picked up her pencil and I picked up my pencil. She wrote *her* name on her piece of paper and I wrote *her* name on my piece of paper. Thus, by mimicking the Chinese girl sitting next to me, I gradually started to learn the ways of American school children.

The English as a Second Language class that started in the middle of my first semester at Garfield Elementary helped me a great deal, but I still hadn't made tremendous progress by the sixth grade when I was enrolled in Mr. Rogers's class. My Mr. Rogers was a lot like the Mr. Rogers on television; gentle, quiet, and concerned about the children around him. He also gave me a book that I have treasured for the rest of my life—*Fifth Chinese Daughter*, by Jade Snow Wong.

Fifth Chinese Daughter is autobiographical, but Jade Snow Wong wrote it when she was in her early twenties, which most people would consider a bit premature for autobiographical material. The book starts early in Jade's life, when she is a young Chinese girl, living with her immigrant parents and siblings in San Francisco's Chinatown. Jade's parents owned a sewing factory and they were very traditional. I think Mr. Rogers thought the book would help me adjust to being Chinese in the American culture, but I didn't understand any deeper levels of the book at that time. For one thing, I still didn't understand enough English to fully appreciate it. I did, however, feel a bond with Jade, because we were both Chinese girls living in Chinatown and because my mother at one point worked in a sewing factory. Much to Mr. Rogers's credit, even that very basic level of understanding provided me with a great deal of comfort at that phase of my life.

Fifth Chinese Daughter then took its place on one of my bookshelves, forgotten and gathering dust for years. I didn't really think about it again until I was a freshman in college at San Jose State University. I was required to take a sociology class, and in that class I had to write a book report about culture. Somehow, I remembered the story of a little girl growing up in Chinatown and I pulled out my old copy of *Fifth Chinese Daughter*. I was genuinely amazed that I now understood the book on a completely different level.

Jade was from a very typical and traditional Chinese family—parents are always right and must be obeyed, no matter what. Family members love each other, of course, but they never openly display this affection. Furthermore, parents put their hopes and dreams in their sons, believing that girls will get married and leave the family. Because Jade's parents feared the corrupting influences of American society, they sent her to a Chinese school. However, they could not afford to support all their children and had to send Jade to live with an American family and attend an American school.

In the American household and at the American school, Jade learns that other children respect their parents, but do not blindly obey. The relationships she observes are much more interactive; children sometimes question and parents sometimes explain. Also, the family is much more demonstrative than her Chinese family.

When Jade returns to her family and questions her parents for the first time, they believe she has adopted dangerous foreign ways. When she tells them she wants to attend college, they tell her she should get married and have children. Jade, however, is very determined. She not only goes to college and studies English, Latin, and chemistry, but she also gets a full scholarship at Mills College and succeeds in science in the 1940s, when girls did not usually study science.

When I read *Fifth Chinese Daughter* in college, I understood that Jade had integrated herself into American society and succeeded. Although my parents were more liberal than her parents, my mother still sent me to Chinese school at a time when I didn't want to be Chinese, I only wanted to be American. I had gone off to college and I was integrating myself into mainstream American society. Again, I identified with Jade and I was surprised at the new layers of the story that I had not appreciated the first time around.

After that book report, *Fifth Chinese Daughter* again took its place on various bookshelves and I did not think about it much until four or five years ago. By that time, I had started to achieve some success with Old Navy, while my husband and I were raising three children. I was very proud of the modern Chinese-American mother I had become. In my eyes, I had become the mother I had always wanted to be; a thoroughly American woman, in touch with my Chinese roots and maintaining the best of my Chinese culture. I visited Hong Kong every year, enjoyed Chinese food, spoke Cantonese, and celebrated Chinese New Year and other major holidays.

Then one day, while attending a mother-daughter tea at my daughter's school, I looked around the room and realized how few Asians there were. When I told my daughter that I'd thought there were more Asians at her school, she told me there were, but that they usually didn't attend this type of function. She explained that this type of function was much more frequently attended by Caucasian parents. What's more, she told me that she thought that I was too American and needed to be more Chinese!

So here I was, thinking of myself as a really hip, Chinese-American mother, who had successfully integrated the two cultures, listening to my fifteen-year-old daughter tell me that she wanted me to be more traditional. At first I argued with her, then I really listened to what she said, which is definitely more of my American side, and realized that she was right. In my bid to become more American, I had forsaken many of the wonderful aspects of Chinese culture.

Fifth Chinese Daughter popped into my head again and I went searching for it on my bookshelves. In rereading it a third time, I realized that although Jade had at first rejected Chinese culture in favor of American culture, she ultimately blossomed into a young adult who was proud of her heritage and sought to truly integrate the two cultures into her life. I really read the book with different eyes and came to understand how much Jade appreciated the beautiful traditions inherent in Chinese culture.

This prompted me to look at my own life and I realized that everything I did outside of my family life had to do with my job and mentoring, and that it was all very Americanized. At the same time I was invited to join the Committee of 100, a group of prominent Chinese from many fields who seek to serve as a bridge between the cultures and systems of Asia and America and provide a forum for issues facing Chinese Americans. Ten years ago, I probably wouldn't have joined this organization, but after rereading *Fifth Chinese Daughter*, I realized that I wasn't fully giving back and focusing on my Chinese roots as I should.

I now feel that I have much more successfully integrated Chinese and American culture into my life (and my daughter agrees). I have also decided to reread *Fifth Chinese Daughter* every five years, to see what new lessons it unveils.

As for Jade Snow Wong, she went on to achieve success both as a writer and as an artist. A mutual friend recently invited me to attend Ms. Wong's eightieth birthday party, but I was unable to, due to prior business engagements. Thinking about this book, however, has inspired me to call my friend and ask to invite Ms. Wong out to lunch. I want to let her know just how much *Fifth Chinese Daughter*, written so many years ago, has comforted me, moved me, and influenced me as it has traveled with me through life.

February 18th, 2004

LIAM NEESON

"He looks at a river and thinks, 'Shall I cast my line here or shall I cast it there?' Just in that decision he seems to describe the state of the human soul."

I came to reading and discovering the power of books quite late in life. I remember joining our little library in my hometown of Ballymena, Northern Ireland, when I was nine or ten. I remember reading a number of children's books and *The Flight of the Heron* about Bonnie Prince Charlie in particular, but none of them really got under my skin.

The first book that did, and it was sort of enforced reading, was Charles Dickens's *David Copperfield*, when I was thirteen or fourteen. I had a very good teacher named Mr. O'Hagan, who read parts of the book to us and got us to read other parts out loud. Dickens just seemed to make these characters, these ridiculous, almost cartoon characters come to life— people like Uriah Heep and Copperfield's stepfather, Mr. Murdstone, a very heavy, bitter, cold-hearted man.

Thinking back to Mr. O'Hagan's class reminded me of the power of Dickens and the power of my discovery of *David Copperfield*, albeit enforced as a part of a course. It really opened a new world for me, an imaginative world of books with the potential to transport you on a great journey as well as give you an amazing education.

David Copperfield really shook up whatever part of my brain works on the creative process for the first time in my life. It opened a door to the discovery of characters and using my imagination. I could see these people from the way Dickens described them; I could almost smell them. I remember the itch I felt, especially when reading *David Copperfield* in class, to jump out of my seat and do impersonations of how Uriah Heep would have walked and how Murdstone would have carried himself.

After that, I became a very regular reader. I tried to get my hands on everything and I read at least one book a week from the library. It was a fantastic springboard, because it sparked my interest in drama and I started going up to audition for parts in school plays shortly thereafter.

Then Shakespeare's *Julius Caesar* got under my skin. I wanted to speak those words, those strange but beautiful cadences Shakespeare had invented. Even though the language was strange, every character was fully described, fully fleshed out in his verse.

I am still an avid reader to this day. As I sit here in my office, I am surrounded by books I haven't read with little yellow sticky notes on them reminding me who recommended the book and why I should read it. The last thing at night, I always try to read something in bed, even if it's only three or four pages, and both Natasha and I take a few books to read whenever we go on vacation.

At the moment, I tend to read fly-fishing books. Nick Lyons is an extraordinary writer of fishing experiences. Like any great writer, he takes what seems to you and me a small experience, a tiny little incident, and turns it into a wonderful, universal topic. He looks at a river and thinks, "Shall I cast my line here or shall I cast it there?" Just in that decision he seems to describe the state of the human soul.

I also enjoy reading to my boys, Daniel and Micheál, who are six and seven. I read to them whenever I can: Dr. Seuss, Celtic legends, Arthurian legends, Native American stories. In listening to these stories, children really learn something about themselves, the power of sharing, and trying to change society for the better. I'm always saying to my boys, books will be your best friends for all of your life and passports to other cultures and worlds.

Daniel and Micheál are still a bit young for the *Harry Potter* books, let alone *David Copperfield*, but it is such a joy for me to watch these new worlds unfold for them, to see the doors open in their minds, to watch them using their imaginations, and to know, hopefully, that reading and books will always play important roles in their lives.

Liam Neeson

January 8th, 2003

GEORGE OLAH

"In fact, I thought little of science before entering university, when I fell in love with chemistry. And who can explain how love happens?"

Albert Einstein was more widely recognizable to Americans than Charlie Chaplin in the 1940s. Why? I think because he looked the part, his wild hair fitting Hollywood's image of a scientist, despite that few understand his science.

Many people think that scientists are different from "normal people." Mysterious creatures, sitting on stools in dark laboratories, hunched over percolating test tubes and Bunsen burners, lost in the recesses of their own minds. In reality, scientists are people; sons and daughters; husbands and wives; fathers and mothers. In short, scientists are just like everyone else in most ways.

Growing up in Central Europe, I was very much like most boys my age. There were yet no computers or televisions, but we had good schools and libraries in Budapest, where my family lived. How I loved wandering through the stacks losing myself among the towering shelves of books and hunting through them. I would set out searching for one book and get distracted by another, which would lead me to another, and so on. All the while, I knew that each of those books held the potential of a new adventure. Cracking the cover and leafing through the pages, entire worlds, both real and imaginary, would unfold.

People often assume that since I am a chemist, I was interested in science from the time I was a child. In fact, I thought little of science before entering university, when I fell in love with chemistry. And who can explain how love happens? Before university, however, I read mostly fiction, literature, history, and later even philosophy.

Winnetou, the Apache Chief, Old Shatterhand, and the other Native American characters in Karl May's novels captivated me as a boy. May wrote more than six hundred books on the Wild West; I don't know that I read them all, but I certainly read every one I could get my hands on.

It is interesting to note that, although Karl May's name is virtually unknown in the United States, he is the best-selling German author to date—current estimates indicate that more than one hundred million copies of his books are in print in more than thirty languages. Boys loved May's books when I was young and I believe they still do. In this more egalitarian era, perhaps girls have fallen in love with his books as well.

Karl May never visited America until well after he published *Winnetou*, and he supposedly never made it west of Buffalo. Perhaps for that reason, his novels are riddled with historical and geographical errors. They are also marked by stereotypes and idealized views of the American West. I didn't know any of that when I was a boy and I'm not sure it would have mattered anyway. I tore through the pages of his books because they were good stories and because they were great adventures. May's America—a land that eventually became my home.

Thinking back on those books, waves of fond memories flow back to me. It also reminds me that whatever people read has the potential to instill in them a love of reading. After that, who knows what marvelous worlds will unfold.

September 24th, 2003

FESS PARKER

"I feel strongly that conclusions drawn relative to the history of our country are incomplete until you have been exposed in detail to the time, energy, money, and blood expended in the name of that history."

In 1930, I was six years old and already an enthusiastic reader. At that tender age, it is of course debatable how much I understood, but my parents encouraged me and my father, in particular, stimulated my reading through the funny papers. He often remembered the interval between Sunday papers with some amusement, since he sometimes had to read them to me more than once.

Later on, at the library in San Angelo, Texas, I discovered a book about Texas's history and its six flags: English, Spanish, French, Mexican, Texas Republic, and the United States. An oil company sponsored the book, which faithfully documented history through extremely good storytelling and interesting drawings, but since Texas had been a confederate state, this may be the first time the concept of political correctness entered my thoughts.

The book had a great deal of influence on me, stimulating my very early interest in history, and I am sure it has had a significant impact on succeeding generations. In rereading it a few years ago, I was pleased to note that time had smoothed the rough edges off of the way people referred to one another and that the slang used during my childhood had disappeared.

In my first grade class, I was perhaps the second best reader. My reading improved significantly between first and second grade because I spent that summer and every other summer until I was sixteen on a farm that belonged to my Grandfather Parker near the little town of De Leon in Comanche County, Texas. When that set of grandparents tired of me, they sent me to a cattle ranch in adjoining Erath County, where my Grandmother Allen and my Uncle Lester raised Hereford cattle.

During the Depression years of the 1930s, the adults were intently focused on making a living and I had to amuse myself. I was lucky enough to have limited access to a radio. What I mean by limited is that the radio ran off an automobile battery, and automobile batteries in 1930s, without generators to recharge them, did not last very long. My grandfather was always suggesting that I was prone to enjoying the radio a bit too much!

Needing to entertain myself while the adults were busy farming and ranching, activities in which I was still too young to participate, I began looking at the books in those agricultural homes and I must say there were not many. There were no Book-of-the-Month clubs then, but I hit the mother lode when I found my father and my Uncle John's high school textbooks. *Huckleberry Finn* and *Tom Brown's Schooldays* excited me, but I think my favorite was *The History of Great Britain*, which must have been written shortly after the twentieth century began. At any rate, I became a fan of history early on and to this day I remain a fan of historical novels such as Stephen Harrigan's recent *The Gates of the Alamo*.

With only books and occasionally the radio to keep me busy (television was not on the scene yet) I was fortunate to be exposed to my grandparents' anecdotal history of growing up in central Texas. Tales of their struggles to make a place for themselves in the center of Texas, not always a hospitable place in those days, were highly entertaining. I loved to sit in my Grandpa Parker's lap and listen while he talked with his friends and I was stunned that they could remember events that had happened twenty-five years earlier. That experience with my grandparents was fundamental in cultivating my appreciation for oral history and the study of history in general.

Following my service in the Navy during World War II, I attended the University of Texas and received my bachelor's degree in American history in 1950. All that being said, it should not surprise anyone that the most exciting and perhaps accurate book of history I have ever read is David McCullough's *John Adams.* The voluminous trove of letters that provided Mr. McCullough with insight into such commonplace details as the weather in January in Braintree, Massachusetts, reflects a heavenly glow on the emotions, character, and deeds of John and Abigail Adams and their family. The hardship of being separated from his wife, family, and friends on behalf of this country and the close calls on the ocean traveling to and from Europe are recounted in gripping detail. We, as Americans, are fortunate that those details and so much more have been saved for posterity in the many, many letters entrusted to the tender care of the State of Massachusetts.

I feel strongly that conclusions drawn relative to the history of our country are incomplete until you have been exposed in detail to the time, energy, money, and blood expended in the name of that history. Mr. Adams's letters paint a vivid picture of the sacrifices one needed to be willing to make for the sake of our young country.

All of my life I had accepted that George Washington and Thomas Jefferson were the premier patriots and founders of our country. However, McCullough's book conveys to me that John Adams is the REAL father of our country. For a book to effectively alter the opinions that I, as an avid reader of historical works, have held for a lifetime is astounding. It is for just that reason that I treasure this particular work.

Fess Parker

November 27th, 2002

MARK PRIOR

"At times, it was hard for me to understand why they insisted that I wouldn't be able to go to baseball practice or play in a game if I didn't finish my homework or do well in school."

My mother is a middle school principal who has been in the San Diego school system for more than thirty-five years. She and my father always stressed the importance of education through high school, college, and even to this day. Reading was always an important component of that education. Consequently, I was raised to believe that books can have a profound impact on our lives.

This really struck home for me when I read Steinbeck's *The Grapes of Wrath*, as a freshman in high school. At the time, I remember thinking that the families in Steinbeck's 1920s were not too different from the middle class families of my world—they were making a living and raising families. But then the 1930s hit and many of those same middle class people lost everything and were reduced to desperate straights by the Depression.

I was already interested in history, and *The Grapes of Wrath* inspired me to learn more about the era depicted in Steinbeck's novel. It also inspired me to learn more about the lives of my family members during that era. For the first time, I asked my grandmother, who is now in her eighties, to really tell me about her childhood. I learned that, unlike Steinbeck's characters, my grandmother's family was relatively lucky, because they owned a small business that supported them through the hard times without any major problems. They didn't lose their house and they weren't kicked off their land. She did, however, clearly remember watching close family friends move away and not understanding why.

Although my parents grew up after the Depression, I think they did a great job helping us to understand that we shouldn't take anything for granted. However, it's easy to believe that everything that has been a constant in your life is the norm and will stay the norm. Reading *The Grapes of Wrath* and learning more about my grandmother's early life helped me to better appreciate what I had and the fact that my parents worked to give me every possible opportunity, both in school and in sports.

At times, it was hard for me to understand why they insisted that I wouldn't be able to go to baseball practice or play in a game if I didn't finish my homework or do well in school. But, I now have a better appreciation of the values my parents were instilling in me; the discipline I have in life and in baseball comes from those values. One of those values is the desire to finish what I start, and this included graduating from college, even through I had already been drafted and had to complete courses around a playing schedule of 162 days a year.

I'm often asked to go to public schools with my teammates and talk to children. Parents tell me that I'm a role model for their children and children tell me that they want to grow up to be just like me. I think this is a big responsibility, and I tell them that being like me includes focusing on their schoolwork and making sure they maximize their educational opportunities. If I hadn't finished my education, I couldn't have demonstrated that I really mean it.

In continuing their education, I hope that these children will develop a passion for books and learning in addition to a passion for sports, just as I did. Then, in their own time, they can discover a book that influences them as much as *The Grapes of Wrath* has influenced me.

August 28th, 2005

AIDAN QUINN

"I felt validated. I was ecstatic. I was alive and I couldn't wait to share it."

My father was an English teacher, and my family moved back and forth between Ireland and the United States. In my house, you couldn't go anywhere without tripping over books by Beckett, O'Casey, Yeats, and all the other great Irish writers. When I was young, however, I was more focused on sports than books and reading. That changed in my teens.

At that time, I literally disappeared into books. My mother even thought there was something wrong with me. She told me that I needed to get out more and socialize, but I was simply lost in the enchanted world of great novels. I couldn't stop—I just couldn't stop.

That period lasted for almost five years. It was the most intense period of reading in my life: I probably read more in those five years than in the ensuing twenty years combined. And the book that really started it, the one that stuck in my head, the one that literally changed my life, was *Notes from Underground,* by Dostoyevsky.

At the time, I was very much an outsider, aligned with the misfits and poets. I loathed all those popular people and, of course, felt guilty about that, because I knew it was ridiculous and that I had my own demons to deal with.

Dostoyevsky's unnamed and unhappy narrator in *Notes from Underground*— the ultimate outsider—seemed to speak directly to me. A minor government worker, he has long, rambling, internal dialogues with himself, during which he insults every one of his superiors, the people he works with, and the popular writers he admires. His negative thoughts fill him with guilt and self-loathing. Surprisingly, for such an angry person, he could also be incredibly generous and soulful. This paradoxical schizophrenia seemed familiar to me; it plugged directly into the angst I was feeling as a teenager.

Notes from Underground was a seminal book in my life, from one of the great writers of all times. I felt like the narrator understood me. But it was more than that, I felt like he understood outsiders in general, humanity, and the human psyche.

I felt validated. I was ecstatic. I was alive and I couldn't wait to share it with one of my best friends, Bill Roberts, because I knew he would love it as well. We would read passages together out loud and laugh uproariously at the mere mortals (similar to the popular folks in high school) the narrator would skewer. I had never reread a book before and, with the exception of *Hamlet*, I have never reread a book since. But I clearly remember rereading *Notes from Underground*.

That was my introduction to Dostoyevsky and I started plowing though his books: *Crime and Punishment, The Idiot, The Brothers Karamazov,* and others. Then I remember thinking, "Oh no, this one is going to end too," so I started to parcel out the reading, twenty-five pages a night to make it last. I really savored those books.

About a year after *Notes from Underground*, I discovered *A Portrait of the Artist as a Young Man*, by James Joyce. It had some of the same themes as *Notes from Underground*, but with the added layers of a world I knew. I had already lived in Dublin, and this was about my tribe.

That period of intense reading certainly influenced my choice of professions. I love storytelling, and as an actor, that's what I'm part of. When I'm lucky enough to be doing a great role that takes an audience on a wonderful journey, I love it. And even though I love acting and I'm in no way belittling it, I sometimes think it's a poor second to what I dreamed of doing: writing.

I always wanted to be the creator of one of those wonderful books, but as a young man, I found that I just didn't have the discipline for the aloneness of it. So I continue to read while somewhere, in the back of my mind and perhaps with a little bit of denial, I still dream about becoming a writer when I grow up.

March 17th, 2003

VANESSA REDGRAVE

"Perhaps this story also gave me hope."

I learned to read when I was four years old. This was during the Second World War, 1940. We had no television, no cinema, and no magazines of any kind. I hated learning to read because the book I learned from was very boring. But then suddenly, I could read, and then I didn't want to stop. The first book I was given was Andrew Lang's *The Blue Fairy Book*.

Then I found a book that had belonged to a sister of my mother's father. *The Pilgrim's Progress: From This World to That Which Is to Come* by John Bunyan. I must have been around six or maybe seven years old. The language was old and difficult, and there were only six or so illustrations. Perhaps because all the men in our family were away fighting Hitler's Nazi occupation of Europe, or in the Pacific fighting the Japanese fascists, John Bunyan's story about Christian's pilgrimage inspired and enthralled me. I especially like the chapter on Vanity Fair. I was excited by the pilgrims' courage and faith in resisting all the worldly temptations, and threats of imprisonment and death.

John Bunyan was a Puritan, and was imprisoned for his beliefs. I did not understand, or know, what Puritanism was. I did not know the history of the times when John Bunyan lived and wrote. I could not understand some of the words he used. But I learned what they meant because I understood his story. Perhaps this story also gave me hope. The times in the war were difficult and horrible for so many people, and I was reassured to learn that "the trumpets sounded for him on the other side" when Christian and his fellow pilgrim crossed the deep and dangerous river.

Vanessa Redgrave

August 15th, 2003

GOVERNOR BILL RICHARDSON

"The book mesmerized me both in a historical and literary sense."

John F. Kennedy wrote *Profiles in Courage* about five years before he was elected president. The book is pure Kennedy—eloquent, informed, and inspirational, with a keen eye toward the force of history.

The book mesmerized me both in a historical and literary sense. It was a senator looking back on the history of the Senate, as punctuated by the institution's most important moments. It was one leader—who later would become one of the world's great voices for freedom and justice—looking at others' courageous stands.

The book is inspiring, not only because it is beautifully written, but also because courage itself is inspiring. Kennedy recognized that inspiration in his book and in his life. As president, perhaps his greatest achievement was to inspire Americans to have courage: the courage to stand up for civil rights, the courage to counteract Soviet aggression, and the courage to believe that we could put a man on the moon.

Profiles in Courage inspired me when I first read it. It continues to inspire me today because I believe that we, as a nation, still need the type of courage from our leaders that Kennedy wrote about. Today we face challenges just as great—challenges to our economic and national security. We also face global challenges, which are shared in common by the people of the world.

As I write this, I am now making my run to become president of the United States. While I cannot claim to share Kennedy's good looks or his Boston Brahmin accent, I do share his belief that we can solve all of our problems. Kennedy once said: "Our problems are man-made, therefore they may be solved by man . . . No problem of human destiny is beyond human beings."

I believe that we truly control our own destiny, and if we have the courage of Kennedy and the leaders he wrote about in *Profiles in Courage*, then the destiny we create for ourselves will restore America to greatness at home and around the world.

William B. Richardson

November 5th, 2007

NATASHA RICHARDSON

"When I read that book it was as if the scales fell from my eyes. It was as if I'd been given the golden key to the door."

I come from a family of readers. I grew up in houses filled with books. Libraries and bookstores were part of my life from a very early age. When my father died, I inherited his extensive book collection, including numerous volumes on everything from American and European history, to politics, to biographies, to books on art and drama, but more importantly, I inherited his love of reading much earlier in life.

My enduring memories of my father are images of him reading. Whenever he wasn't actively directing a film, he would spend most afternoons in his house in Los Angeles reading. It was a very important activity for him, not just something he did because he had nothing else to do, but something that was a true joy.

That same love of reading has always stayed with me. In England, students sit for O-Level exams when they are sixteen and A-Level exams to get into college. When I was studying for my O-Levels and should have been doing my homework, I was reading one trashy novel after the other. I remember reading for hours on end. In fact, I read so much that I didn't get very good grades on my exams. That kind of book wouldn't interest me now, but then it was completely consuming.

When I was at drama school, I felt that my education wasn't giving me the clues I was looking for or the tools I needed to become the actress I wanted to be. The teaching was quite old-fashioned and it wasn't really the drama school of my dreams. Then my mother recommended I read Stanislavski's *An Actor Prepares*. When I read that book it was as if the scales fell from my eyes. It was as if I'd been given the golden key to the door. Suddenly, I saw that there was a method, a way of working that not only made total sense to me intellectually, but which also made sense in my heart and in my soul.

An Actor Prepares is a handbook that really only describes what most good actors do anyway, but it gave me a real approach to the work and a reminder of basic groundwork. I'll never forget the principal of the drama school's reaction when I knocked on his door and said, "I'm so excited because I found this book and now everything seems clear." He was so dismissive and replied, "Oh you want to be careful of that." Needless to say, I didn't heed his advice, and that method became the foundation stone for my work as an actress and it's something that I've been able to go back to across the years.

There was a period when I just read so much, that it's difficult to remember all the books, but in addition to Dickens and the Brontës, two great classic books have always stayed with me: Elizabeth Gaskell's *Wives and Daughters* and George Eliot's *Daniel Deronda*. They are both romantic novels that deal with love, but they are also very socially conscious. They are very much of their time and incisive on the problems of poverty, illiteracy, racism, and sexism and how those issues inform the characters in those novels.

I read *Wives and Daughters* years and years ago, but it has always stayed with me, because it somehow resonated with me. Elizabeth Gaskell wrote in a very modern way about women in a very closed society. The repression of people's souls is an enduring theme, an illuminating one that lives through the ages, whether it be the oppression people feel as a society, as an individual, because of a bad relationship, or because of economic circumstances and class restrictions.

I fell in love with *Daniel Deronda*. My mother did a play based on the novel when she was a young actress and she recommended I read it. I thought it would make the most marvelous film, but I also realized that it was an epic on such a huge scale that it wouldn't be possible without a major director who could take on Victorian England and the whole world of Jewish people and Judaism in England at the time. I felt enormously for the heroine, Gwendolen, and I've always wanted to play her. Gwendolen is a spoiled rich girl whose time is running out on the possibility of marriage, in an age when women who didn't find a husband were thrown onto the rubbish heap of life with few options other than becoming a governess or a virtual servant living in a rich relative's home. Gwendolen takes the wrong course and falls for a rich man who sets out to destroy her. Finally, through the redemption of the novel, she realized the horror of the path she has taken and regrets all the decisions she's made.

I used to go to the bookstores every week and buy whatever interesting book came out that week. Unfortunately, since I've had children, there doesn't seem to be as much time to read. Nevertheless, there is always something about picking up a book that can transport me into another world of people's hearts and minds and help me understand things in ways I hadn't before. Now that I have less time, reading is no longer something I take for granted, but something that is one of the biggest treats in my life.

And of course, one of the great joys of having children is watching them learn to read and discover the world of books. My sons have both read since the age of five, but they have always preferred picture books. Last night for the first time Micheál, who is seven, proudly showed me the *Star Wars* paperback he was reading by his bed lamp. As he sat there with his little bookmark, he told me he'd bought it at Barnes & Noble and that he was going to buy the next one when he finished.

I don't think we should dictate what people should and shouldn't read. I think we should simply encourage them to read. As long as my son, or anyone else for that matter, is picking up a book on his own and as long as he wants to buy the next one, he is learning and evolving. If someone enjoys any book, it has potential to lead him or her to something more substantial in the future.

December 10th, 2002

CARTER ROBERTS

"I believe that imagination and persistence are the most important traits we bring to our work, because we must have the ability to imagine the world differently."

"The night Max wore his wolf suit and made mischief of one kind and another, his mother called him WILD THING."
—Maurice Sendak, *Where the Wild Things Are*

I first read these words—the opening line of Maurice Sendak's classic *Where the Wild Things Are*—when I was eight years old, and I was transfixed. I was drawn into the story of Max and his adventures, and when I closed my eyes I knew I could see how "that very night, in Max's room, a forest grew, and grew and grew—until his ceiling hung with vines and the walls became the world all around."

Where the Wild Things Are is all about imagination—the magnificent power to imagine differently our world and our role in it. Max can create the world in which he lives that night, because he can imagine it. In fact, at World Wildlife Fund (WWF), I believe that imagination and persistence are the most important traits we bring to our work, because we must have the ability to imagine the world differently, and we must persist in creating change.

There is so much bad news and the problems we face are so big and so complex that it is easy to despair. Each and every day we read about the seemingly insurmountable problems the world faces—from war to genocide; from pollution to global warming; and, from the collapse of the world's fisheries and deforestation, to extinction faced by tens of thousands of species around the globe.

In the midst of all these problems, we see that people can and do make a difference through imagining and creating new solutions. One can easily believe that institutions are too rigid or inflexible to change. And, yet, they can and they do change; governments and corporations adapt and behave in more sustainable ways with greater conscience all the time. One can easily believe that people cannot live in harmony with nature in certain areas of the world. And, yet, we find that, given the proper tools and resources, people are the best guardians of their local environments and the species that live in them.

At WWF, more than five million people in more than one hundred countries make a difference in changing the world through their membership in our organization. I am confident that we can solve problems with creative solutions—whether it's imagining a different way of producing soy in Brazil that preserves the rainforest, or imagining a new marine reserve off the coast of Mozambique that enables people to catch more fish, or imagining a future in which we live more efficiently as a society. The act of imagination is fundamental to what we're trying to do with this organization.

Imagining our world differently and adapting our behavior enables us to avoid the disasters faced by societies past and present. No book better depicts those scenarios than *Collapse*, published by Jared Diamond in 2005—the same year I became president and CEO of WWF. In his seminal book, Jared highlights what happens to societies that don't imagine their world differently and don't adapt to change—from Easter Island to the Vikings of Greenland, and from the Maya of Central America to modern-day China. In each of those four stories we see four factors that led to the utter collapse and disappearance of some of the most notable civilizations on Earth: destruction of their natural environment, climate change, hostile neighbors, and friendly trade partners.

When I finished reading *Collapse*, my first reaction was resolve—the resolution to make clear the extent to which people depend on nature and all the different ways that the environment supports our basic livelihoods in the United States and around the world. We must make that connection clear to people so that we act before it's too late.

If, for example, China simply catches up to the United States in its consumption patterns, we will require twice as much oil and twice as many minerals as the world produces today. If the rest of the world catches up to the United States, it will require thirteen times as much.

Collapse is ultimately a morality tale illustrating, in detail, how much we, as a society, utterly depend on the environment for food, climate, and quality of life. It also paints a dramatic picture of the consequences of not taking action. Unless we as a society learn to adapt and change, we may very well go the way of Easter Island, or the Maya.

There is reason to choose optimism over despair. First, since these problems are caused by humans, it remains within our power to solve them. Second, there have been many successes, including species brought back from the brink of extinction. In the 1930s and 1940s, due mostly to the illegal trade in animal parts, the population of the Siberian tiger living in the wild had plummeted to approximately thirty. Today we estimate that there are 450 of these magnificent animals in the wild, and their population continues to grow.

I recently visited our work in Mozambique, where we are helping local communities create and manage marine resources, which is leading to a dramatic return of their fisheries and their availability of food. Based on these examples, I can imagine solutions. I can imagine a world that places greater value on these species and their habitat than the short-term economic gain from poaching and deforestation. I can imagine governments engaged in conservation, corporations engaged in sustainable practices, and local populations, who have a deep understanding of ecosystems, actively engaged in protecting them.

What is the alternative? Of course we want our children to experience the joy of books and reading so they can imagine new and wonderful worlds. We also want them to see and experience the extraordinary planet where we live—a planet of clean rivers and tropical rainforests, coral reefs teeming with fish, ecosystems supporting people's livelihoods and creatures as strange and wonderful as those seen by Max in *Where the Wild Things Are*.

October 4th, 2009

"My most enduring nonprofessional interest, however, has been in both factual history and historical fiction and, as I've grown older, I've gone back further in time."

I began first grade at the age of five, and skipped the fourth grade, so from then I was always two years younger than my classmates. I entered the ninth grade when I was twelve, was fifteen during my senior year of high school, and entered college the week following my sixteenth birthday. In terms of interests, this age gap often separated me from my classmates.

In many ways, I was a loner, but I was a loner in the midst of many people. I played basketball and tennis on the high school teams, was on the debate team, but my interests were often different from the interests of most people with whom I shared classrooms. Part of that difference simply stemmed from the fact that they were older, but part of it also arose from the fact that I was interested in topics and reading material that nobody else was reading. These topics would never come up in conversation. And school was very different then than it is now. I walked to grade school every day, went home for lunch and then went back to school. In junior high, I had a paper route delivering the *Columbus Dispatch*, every afternoon, but still rode my bicycle home for lunch, about four city blocks, all during my high school years.

Fortunately, I could explore my interests at Ohio Wesleyan University's library, because my father's position as a professor of mathematics led the librarians to grant me access to the stacks when I was twelve or thirteen. (When I became a freshman at OWU, my access was withdrawn because freshmen were by rule not given "stack access" until their sophomore year!) I spent many days wandering through those stacks of books and newspapers, randomly reading whatever caught my attention. I read a lot of history, mostly within the previous century or two, and I often found myself also leaning toward popular material that included quantitative data.

I suppose I always thought I would become a scientist, because I enjoyed working with numbers, which came easily for me, and I knew that science was a profession that would allow me to do just that. I did not, however, read more widely in science than in any other topic back then. If anything, I leaned toward history and factual documents, following the historical trail wherever it led.

When I was twelve or thirteen, my journeys through the stacks led me to the 1904-1905 issues of the *New York Times*. In 1904, the Japanese wiped out the Russian Pacific fleet in the opening days of the Russo-Japanese War. Russia then sent its Baltic fleet around the world to Japan, where it too was destroyed in one of the most decisive naval defeats in history.

The Russian fleet's progress around the world from the Baltic to the Asian coast was chronicled in the *New York Times*. Even though I already knew how the story ended, I found it interesting to watch history unfold in the yellowed pages of those newspapers. Those articles were part of an interest in battleships and naval warfare. I'm not quite sure why I was so intrigued by this topic, since I lived in landlocked central Ohio and I'd never seen a ship, but I was. I then came across the two-volume *Battleships in Action*, by H. W. Wilson, which chronicles naval warfare from the late Civil War through World War I, and I read it in great detail.

In September of 1941, three months before Pearl Harbor, my father, who had been a field artillery officer in France during World War I, and in the Army Reserves between wars, was called into active duty. He wasn't returned to civilian life until March 1946, so I followed the war very closely. It quickly became apparent that naval wars were not won with ships; they were won with aircraft. As a result, my close interest in battleships waned.

Shortly after Pearl Harbor, stories started to appear which essentially stated that the Japanese as an ethnic group were quite unintelligent. During one of my forays into the university library, I decided to investigate if that assertion were true, or if it was just propaganda. I found the results of IQ tests done in California during the 1930s and learned that people of Japanese descent actually scored slightly higher than average, rather than well below average.

For me, in retrospect, that incident, and others like it, highlighted the importance and the power of reading for oneself. I could push around in a sea of information and find facts, rather than accepting someone else's word. I could see the basis on which the conclusion was drawn and draw a conclusion of my own, which might not be the same. This habit is obviously very important to all scientists as they sift through apparently conflicting pieces of information.

When I became a graduate student, we knew the article that you should have read, but hadn't, was probably written in German or perhaps French, and we were examined by the chemistry department on our ability to read those languages. By the 1960s and 1970s, with a vast increase in the amount of published science, a large fraction of it in English, the valuable-but-not-yet-read article was probably in English. There was simply too much information and the problem has steadily gotten worse. Today, the instrumentation in science is so fantastically capable that we are all swamped by the sheer magnitude of available data, but it also provides answers to questions that couldn't be answered fifty years, or even ten years ago. In fact, for at least the last four hundred years, there has been a tremendous scientific advance every fifty years.

Even as this ever-expanding sea of information allows us to explore increasingly complex and interesting problems, it forces us to focus, because there is no end to the reading and research we could do. And, I believe the general perception outside is that we scientists probably read about science all the time, but I don't and many other scientists do not either.

When I come home, I enjoy reading magazines, such as the *Atlantic Monthly,* the *Columbia Journalism Review,* the *New York Review of Books,* the *Economist,* and the weeklies like *Newsweek* and *U.S. News.* I also enjoy fiction, including Tony Hillerman's detective novels set in the Southwest, which my wife and I buy in hardback as soon as they are released. She is an omnivorous reader, which I suppose I am, too, but a lot of my reading must still be from *Science* and *Nature* and the geophysical and chemical literature. My most enduring nonprofessional interest, however, has been in both factual history and historical fiction and, as I've grown older, I've gone back further in time.

Recently, my interest in naval warfare and life on the sea was rekindled through the novels of Patrick O'Brien, based on the British Navy in the 1800s. The first time I started reading in the series, which eventually ended with twenty volumes, I jumped right into the middle around number ten, and didn't really get caught up in the book. Then, about a year later, I decided to try again, starting at the beginning. All of the books have separate endings, but the main characters are always there, and it is a sequence that builds. This time, I enjoyed the first book very much and immediately started the second. After reading a few more in rapid succession, I was afraid that I was getting through them too fast, so I decided to parcel them out and I'm still, gradually, enjoying the series. I have a colleague who went through all twenty books rather quickly. He is now, because the author has died, about to start through the series again.

Sometimes, I think my wife wonders why I read so much about military affairs and naval warfare, but they are topics that have interested me ever since I read the old news clippings in the stacks at the Ohio Wesleyan University library. I think that this demonstrates the importance of reading, and the way in which the habits of reading in childhood or adolescence carry over into an interest that can last a lifetime.

F. Sherwood Rowland

January 20th, 2004

"Is it possible in your heart to believe that a person is more than the worst thing he does?"

I have always been against the death penalty, because it struck me as arbitrary, capricious, expensive, and not an effective deterrent. However, I had no visceral connection with the issue until I read *Dead Man Walking*, by Sister Helen Prejean.

Dead Man Walking really got to me on two levels. The strange and horrific specifics of the death penalty interested me at the time. However, the larger issue—this strange love story between a nun and the two men she ultimately serves as spiritual advisor—is what really moved me.

The hook in the book for me was the question of unconditional love and the journey that this person, Sister Helen, went on without understanding where it was leading her. While reading the book, I fell in love with Sister Helen because of the mistakes she made. She didn't enter into her role as spiritual advisor to two death-row inmates convicted of rape and murder thinking that she had the answers. In fact, she was terrified as she entered a very dark place and she questioned herself the entire way. Her journey, starting out by writing a letter to someone and going deeper and deeper, one step at a time, is very powerful.

Somewhere deep inside of herself, Sister Helen knew what was right and she listened to that voice. Day by day, she made the difficult decision to move toward the light and not toward the darkness. Only in hindsight, looking back along the path she had traveled, did she see the answers more clearly. Reading about her ability to keep moving forward, even though she was terrified, even though it was painful, and even though it cost her so much personally and emotionally, really inspired me.

I also started to have a visceral reaction to the death penalty that I hadn't had before. This reaction resulted in part from Sister Helen's brilliant portrayal of all victims affected by this issue—not just the victims of the crimes, and not just the people the state murders, but the families, the warden, and all the people forced to be a part of a system that premeditatively kills another human being. Along the way, she raises questions. Is it possible to take into account the most despicable act of a human being and still find a way to love him? Is it possible in your heart to believe that a person is more than the worst thing he does? These are powerful, universal questions that really struck me.

I was working on *The Client* while reading *Dead Man Walking*, and we went to New Orleans for a week to film. When I learned that Sister Helen would also be there, I asked to meet her. I hadn't really thought about turning the book into a movie, because great books don't always make great movies. I simply wanted to meet her because I was so intrigued by her and I was very moved by her book.

Sister Helen didn't really know who I was, other than one of the two girls in *Thelma & Louise*, but I had come highly recommended by some people I'd worked with in Amnesty International over the years. I also didn't know what to expect. Although I'd had a great deal of exposure to nuns over the years, it wasn't necessarily positive. I went to a Catholic grammar school and I went to a Catholic university in the late '60s, when a lot of young priests were running off with the nuns. I didn't think the Church was particularly practical for many reasons—women's role on the bottom of the food chain, the Church's stance on reproductive rights and other issues, and its wealth, in such stark contrast to so many poor people the world over.

As a result of my past experience, I had lost any love of organized religion, and it was wonderful to meet someone who had found a way to be connected to the world and still have her faith. Many independent nuns like Sister Helen became radicalized and politicized, because it can't be helped when working in poor communities. That is certainly true of the Church all over the world, but we don't see much of it in the United States.

During that first meeting, Sister Helen and I developed an immediate bond and started talking about the possibility of turning the book into a movie. She gave me the rights then and there. We didn't even sign anything. She just asked what we should do, and my agent later spoke to her book agent.

I thought it would be a wonderful project for my then partner. Over the course of the next year, Sister Helen came often to New York and stayed with us. Our friendship grew deeper and deeper, but Tim still hadn't really looked at the book. Finally, I told Tim that we should probably give it to someone else if he wasn't interested. He read it, and little by little it started to get into his imagination, and then he started to write it. Eventually, it won out over *Cradle Will Rock*, which was made after *Dead Man Walking*.

This type of film is obviously not a documentary, so there has to be some liberty taken in terms of how the story is told. Everything is about the director's point-of-view, how he tells the story, and what he chooses to emphasize, and Tim had some brilliant ideas. We couldn't have two executions, so he consolidated the two men into one character. He also decided to change the execution to lethal injection—the men in the book were electrocuted—but he spoke with Sister Helen about it first. She was very much involved in how the story unfolded in the film.

For me, playing a real person is an enormous responsibility, especially if that person is still alive and a close friend. Then there is the problem of dealing with an issue that is really close to your heart. I didn't realize until we were finished filming just how stressful it was, because I wanted to make sure the story was told the way it deserved to be. Consequently, I felt an enormous relief when Sister Helen liked the film and approved of it.

Initially, we had hoped that the story would at least exist on tape to help people understand the death penalty in a very specific, rather than a purely theoretical way. I think we achieved even more than that and it's always shocking to me when I meet young kids who tell me that they have seen *Dead Man Walking* a number of times—it's not a very easy movie to watch. I assume it's very satisfying for Sister Helen as well to know the conversation the film has encouraged.

Dead Man Walking changed my life in many ways. It brought Sister Helen into my life. I love her very much, and we've grown even closer over time. I've continued to be involved in issues concerning the death penalty and I occasionally have the opportunity to work with Sister Helen to promote understanding of the issue, or to raise funds to support abolitionist groups. It also provided a wonderful opportunity for me to work on something with Tim that turned out very well.

The book and the movie serve as tools that are used to begin a dialogue about the death penalty. Now, when Sister Helen speaks, thousands of people turn out instead of hundreds. The book, which was number one on the *New York Times* Best Seller List for thirty-one weeks, was subsequently translated into ten different languages and even went to the Vatican.

I now understand that the question is not, "Who deserves to die?" The question is "Who deserves to kill?" Sister Helen's book helped me understand this question and I feel it with every fiber of my body.

December 16th, 2016

MARTIN SCORSESE

"At other times, he gives us an adventure novel. Then, a patch of philosophizing. Then, a little documentary about how things work."

The room where Herman Melville wrote *Moby-Dick* can be found on the top floor of his home in Pittsfield, Massachusetts. When you look out the window, you can clearly see the top of Mount Greylock, which many have said suggests the shape of a great white whale. It certainly seems plausible enough. And the image of Melville sitting at his desk, pausing from his work and gazing out at this particular view seems so much in the spirit of the book itself. To gaze . . . to contemplate . . . *Moby-Dick* is, after all, an act of contemplation, a long, hard look into the eye of life. Melville found something there, something as solid and immovable as a mountain. Can we call it "evil" and leave it at that? As with all great works of art, Melville's novel cannot be reduced to a central thesis or point. Nor can it be stripped down or retold as an adventure story. That's why it's never been made into a fully satisfying film. It has to be experienced, chapter by chapter, word by word.

Many people have commented on the grandeur of Melville's language in *Moby-Dick*. Would you call it poetic? Musical? Shakespearean? Biblical? It's all of those things, but of course it has its own gravity and power. And somehow it's a distinctly American voice. It helps if your ear has been tuned to Shakespeare, but the knotted brilliance of Melville's language could only have come out of New England. It has to do with the severity, the reach back to Puritanism, the sense of a harsh, avenging God. You feel the same thing in Hawthorne's writing, but where Hawthorne is ethereal—his stories strike like lightning and then disappear into the night—Melville is as hard and solid as stone. All I know is that I found the language enthralling when I read the novel for the first time, and that it's always excited me when I've returned to it over the years.

Something else I've always found so exciting about *Moby-Dick* is the way the story is told. At times, Melville gives us a very sharp character study. At other times, he gives us an adventure novel. Then, a patch of philosophizing. Then, a little documentary about how things work on a whaling boat. Melville was fearless about bending structure, taking the reader down a variety of different paths, each one as absorbing as the other. This approach has always felt very lifelike to me. We rarely look at any experience, whether it's walking down the street or visiting a foreign country, from a single viewpoint. We consider everything from a variety of viewpoints. I've always been attracted to this kind of storytelling, in film and in literature, and it's one of the many elements that make *Moby-Dick* so enduring.

But most of all, it's the darkness of Melville's vision that I find so compelling. The question of good and evil is always a very difficult one. At this point in history, at least in this country, the concepts of "good" and "evil" have become clichés, labels for things we like and things we don't like. But then, of course, the *real* question of evil is always with us. It shadows us. Because when we read that eight hundred thousand people have been killed in Rwanda, we can't really say that "they" did it—at least not in an ultimate sense. Of course people say this all the time, but we all know that there is no such thing as "they." It is *us*. It has always *been* us. Hawthorne understood this but Melville went beyond understanding—he absorbed it, and wrestled with it. On the page. And, it goes without saying, in his life. It's difficult to imagine how painful it must have been.

The whiteness of the whale. The terror of that whiteness, a terror that can make you almost giddy because there's no end to it, there's no knowing it, or understanding it. It's just *there*. Always. And then, the darkness of Ahab, an almost physical reaction against a world that could house something like *Moby-Dick*. A different kind of terror. I suppose you could call it the terror of folly. Many people choose to believe that evil can actually be eliminated or removed from the world. You hear it every day on the radio, you read it in the papers, you see it on television. Is it naive to believe such a thing? I would say, rather, that it's human. Tragically so.

I immediately connected with *Moby-Dick*. In fact, it was one of the very first novels I read. Melville may have been writing about a whaling vessel out of New Bedford in the 1850s, but the essence of his novel reflected what I was seeing every day on the streets of New York, one hundred years later. The same sense of folly in the face of existence, the same feeling of rage, reducing people to hollow shells. It's a part of us. I don't know that we'll ever rid ourselves of the moral vanity that Melville confronted here. I suppose that his unflinching gaze would be a good place to start.

I've always been haunted by the last lines of *Moby-Dick*, and they continue to haunt me as I think of them now. Ishmael has survived the shipwreck and finds himself floating in the water, grasping a "coffin life-buoy." Sharks swim past him and hawks fly overhead, but they don't go near him—it's as if he's been blessed—or cursed. "On the second day, a sail drew near, nearer, and picked me up at last. It was the devious-cruising *Rachel*, that in her retracing search after her missing children, only found another orphan."

Melville had it sadly, terribly right. We imagine that we're someone's child, but in the end we're all orphans. Tragic. But maybe, just maybe, liberating.

July 7th, 2004

SRI SRI RAVI SHANKAR

"When knowledge lodges in one's intellect as one's own experience, it becomes living wisdom."

Everyone's life is like a book and every book is infused with the consciousness of the writer. It is important that we don't perceive books as static or cognitive objects, but as living sources of connectivity beyond time and space. The ancient people revered books as living entities. Even today if you visit any Sikh temple, it is the book which is the Deity or the Master. It is the source of faith. Books not only authenticate one's experience, but also open infinite possibilities for the future, broaden one's horizon, and heighten one's consciousness.

Capturing the knowledge in books has enabled humankind to progress in science, medicine, philosophy, and in fact supported human evolution as a whole. Amusement, wonder, humor, and all such positive emotions are kindled by books. The wise one spends time in science, arts, music, charity, and celebration. The foolish one spends time in lamenting, regretting, grieving, and blaming oneself and others.

Books can engross you and take you into a different world altogether. Before and during my teens, I used to walk two kilometers to get to the library, and I found it very difficult to choose books as my interest was diverse. Literature, science, philosophy, poetry, and history were all equally interesting for me. I could never read much, just a few paragraphs would take me into meditation. When I walked back home, I would be contemplating on what I had read and I would even walk past my home sometimes.

Reading is complete only when you assimilate the ideas and contemplate on it. If you simply read a book without retaining anything, it is a waste of time. There are those who take pride saying they have not read anything and there are others who spent all the time in memorizing scriptures. Neither of them attains wisdom.

Yoga Vasistha is one book which has great wisdom about consciousness and various dimensions of life. When knowledge lodges in one's intellect as one's own experience, it becomes living wisdom. In fact, the definition of a teacher in the Upanishads is "Shotriam Brahmanishtam"; a Master is one whose reading is coupled with experience.

Reading or swadhyaya, self-study, is one of the rules of a civilized society. I often recommend that people read subjects in which they are not proficient. For example, a poet should not read others' poems, but rather read some other subjects such as history, art, or science. Similarly, a painter could read poetry or listen to music. Such study can strengthen one in different dimensions, broaden perspectives, and help with true creativity and innovation. Every child should grow up reading a little bit about all the religions of the world. This can help one appreciate different viewpoints from an early age and this will be like a vaccination against radicalization, the biggest problem in the world today.

December 5th, 2016

EUNICE KENNEDY SHRIVER

"She changed the attitudes of the world with regard to the poor, the dying, and the ill. She, more than any other figure in history, showed the power of love put into action."

Mother Teresa knew that "love has no meaning if it isn't shared. Love has to be put into action." I would like to imitate Mother Teresa in her extraordinary examples of love in action for the people most often overlooked, neglected, and underestimated in our society—those persons with intellectual disabilities. I invariably find inspiration, motivation, and courage from Mother Teresa's book *A Simple Path*.

In her book, Mother Teresa talks about the variety of programs she created to allow her to serve her community—the poorest of the poor, the sick and the dying in India. She created Shishu Bhavan—a home for orphan children; Prem Nivas, a home for leprosy patients; Nirmal Hriday—a home for the dying and destitute; and Prem Dan—a home for TB sufferers and patients with intellectual disabilities. Through these services, she found a way to address the needs of the underserved community in its entirety around the world. Mother Teresa's impact went far beyond those individuals she served. She changed the attitudes of the world with regard to the poor, the dying and the ill. She, more than any other figure in history, showed the power of love put into action—showed that it can transform the giver as much as the receiver, showed that "one act—one attitude—one person at a time" is the path to global change, and I draw inspiration from that every day of my life.

In creating Special Olympics, we sought to provide opportunities for friendship, sports, education, and jobs for people with intellectual disabilities. In 1962, I started a sports camp—Camp Shriver—for children with intellectual disabilities in my backyard because I was outraged that my community did not offer any services or sports for our neighbors with intellectual disabilities. One of the most heart-warming images I can think of is the determined face of a courageous child with a disability learning to swim and the resulting joy of her mother as she witnesses the capabilities of her child. The effect was not only of improving the lives of the children and their families who participated in Camp Shriver, but also of changing the attitudes of the whole community and showing the world that these are people deserving of love and care. This was the beginning of a critical shift in the way the world relates to people with intellectual disabilities, showing that by changing attitudes—you can change the world.

The largest disability group in the world is people with intellectual disability. There are 170 million people with intellectual disability around the world. They have suffered and continue to suffer the most unmentionable indignities. Think now for a moment, of those in South Africa who sit alone unclothed in a cold institution; of those in Russia who will never put on a backpack to go to school; of those in Washington, DC, who cry at night because they don't understand why they don't have friends. And think, too, of their parents—think of the mother who loves her special child but who feels so desperately alone. Think of the family that cannot participate in the economy because of the demands of caring for a disabled son or daughter. They have done nothing wrong, committed no crime, and perpetuated no injustice. They are the world's most innocent victims, and they have suffered all this only because they are different. Someone else thinks they don't matter. Someone else thinks they can't participate in our community life. Someone else thinks they should be pushed aside.

We do not believe they should be pushed aside. All in my family have dedicated their lives to eradicate this injustice in the world, and continue to fight for, and with, those with intellectual disabilities. President Kennedy established what is now called the Centers for Excellence in Disability, with a focused mission on training medical professionals and educators for service to those with disabilities, and secured funding for the creation of the National Institute of Child Health and Human Development, the world's first research center dedicated to medical and psychological aspects of intellectual disabilities. Senator Kennedy continues to carry this torch in Congress as he advocates for increased funding and services for those with intellectual disabilities.

Following the examples of their uncles and their parents, my own children have integrated Mother Teresa's dictum of social change—love in action—into their daily lives and the lives of their children. Bobby has raised millions of dollars on behalf of Special Olympics. Mark continues to provide foundation connections that have brought funding and collaboration opportunities to Special Olympics programs around the world. Anthony created Best Buddies, an organization that builds friendships between people with and without intellectual disability. Maria has authored children's books (*What's Wrong with Timmy?*) and traveled to many countries with her husband, Arnold, as Ambassadors for Special Olympics to educate the public on the topic of disabilities. All their lives are inspired by their friends with intellectual disabilities, because they have focused on making a difference in their families, their community, and the world. And now their children have accepted the call to action themselves, participating in Camp Shriver 2004, starting Unified Sports teams for children with and without intellectual disabilities, becoming a Best Buddy, and volunteering for Special Olympics.

Special Olympics answers the call for change and provides opportunities and sports training in over 150 countries and every state in the United States. Under my son, Dr. Timothy Shriver's leadership, Special Olympics has grown and now reaches nearly two million athletes and six million families worldwide. It has expanded to include the Special Olympics Healthy Athletes Program—a resource for athletes to learn about good health practices and nutrition—and SO Get Into It, a school curriculum teaching the importance of acceptance, diversity, and inclusion of our special students, reaching 1.3 million students in over 3,500 schools in sixty countries around the world.

However, there is still more work to be done. Whether you are a coach, a mother, or a young student, or the president of the United States, the call to action is the same: Put your love into action. As Timothy has said so eloquently, "to unlock opportunity, to discover ability, to celebrate giftedness, to welcome every person" in your own backyards, in your schools, in your sports fields, in your places of employment—then you too can put love into action and follow Mother Teresa's example.

Eunice Kennedy Shriver

February 1st, 2005

SENATOR ALAN K. SIMPSON

"If you are only interested in the life of politics, it is a
barbaric existence. I also need art, music, and books."

I didn't even really speak until I was two-and-one-half years old. Hard to believe, I know! I didn't have to because my dear brother Pete, thirteen months my senior, spoke for me. He would say, "Al is hungry," or "Al wants to go to bed," or "Al wants to get down."

Even though I didn't catch on to speech until a little later in life, I always enjoyed books. I remember curling up close as my mother and father read to Pete and me. We would look at the pictures, always-marvelous pictures: *Treasure Island* illustrated by N. C. Wyeth, *Poems of Childhood* illustrated by Maxfield Parrish, and so many more. As we grew older the pictures blended with the text and we moved on to the books of L. Frank Baum, books like *Sky Island*, which he wrote before the *Oz* series.

I remember reading Rudyard Kipling in my teens and being particularly struck by his poem, "If." It ends with, "If you can fill the unforgiving minute / With sixty seconds' worth of distance run, / Yours is the Earth and everything that's in it, / And—which is more—you'll be a Man, my son!" I have found a great deal of meaning in that poem and wherever I teach, I tell my students to reread "If" every five years or so and I know they will find new meaning every time they read it.

Reading is something I have always cherished. Reading is the key to an active life, the salvation from boredom, and it has made me what I am today. Why? Because reading opened my mind to the curiosity, imagination, and adventure that have lasted me a lifetime. I am always deeply saddened when I read statistics about the astounding rates of illiteracy among prisoners and those on death row. I often wonder how different their lives might have been if someone had taught them to read.

Recently, Ann and I attended the Lab School gala in Washington, DC. This school teaches children with learning disabilities and each year the school honors several role models . . . people—corporate CEOs, celebrities, politicians—who could not read because they had learning disabilities, such as dyslexia. They just didn't see things the way other children did.

The kids who attend the Lab School often ask the honorees questions such as, "Were you called a dummy?" And the honorees often reply, "Was I called a dummy? I wasn't only called a dummy, my teachers used to whack me on the hand and place a 'dunce cap' on my head." It's fascinating to hear these stories of those who have succeeded and those stories greatly motivate the kids. Perhaps certain prisoners in our penal system had learning disabilities that were never addressed, or perhaps they just never had positive role models.

I am not dyslexic, but I could never diagram a sentence to save my life! I used to dread the moment the teacher would write a sentence on the board, hand me a piece of chalk, and ask me to diagram it. I could pick out the nouns and adjectives pretty well. I was great at adjectives and I still am! The verbs were a small problem, but once it descended into the depths of adverbs and dangling participles, I was completely lost. It was like reading an Egyptian novel to me; I just couldn't understand one shred of it and I had to go into a remedial English class in college.

Fortunately for me, in addition to the wonderful support of my parents, I had dedicated teachers who encouraged me to read. My own imagination and curiosity continued to grow and these twin traits have held me in good stead ever since.

If you are only interested in the life of politics, it is a barbaric existence. I also need art, music, and books. Sometimes in a deadly hearing or a day of absolutely stupefying details, I could imagine myself fishing on our beloved Bobcat Ranch, like James Thurber's Walter Mitty, who could imagine himself a great surgeon while sitting quietly in a car waiting for his wife. Imagination clears the mind. It gives me the power to look at something and wonder what it does, where it came from, how it flies . . . or how it functions. I can't invent anything . . . hell, I can't even drive a nail! But imagination helps me to think I'm a wizard, a marvelous wizard!

To this day, when I see a Maxfield Parrish or an N. C. Wyeth painting, I am transported back, back to those pleasant times of cozying up to my mother and father as they read to my dear brother and me. Those are fuzzy, tender memories and I'm very lucky to have them down inside to carry with me through life. Reading did that.

February 28th, 2003

SHARON STONE

"The refinding of this and several other books was a re-finding of myself."

"Being an artist means: not numbering and counting, but ripening like a tree, which doesn't force its sap, and stands confidently in the storms of spring, not afraid that afterward summer may not come. It does come. But it comes only to those who are patient, who are there as if eternity lay before them, so unconcernedly silent and vast."
—Rainer Maria Rilke, *Letters to a Young Poet*

This quote is just one of many quotes from *Letters to a Young Poet* by Rainer Maria Rilke that inspires me. Although this is a small book—a compilation of ten letters written by Rilke to a student between 1903 and 1908—it is filled with ageless wisdom.

The hardest times, when we look back through history, are also when people are closest to each other, because they are forced to rely on one another to get through. These are the times when we find our strengths, not just as individuals, but also as a community.

We are in very difficult times now, for many reasons. But we're also in a time that can be very inspirational. I have also been going through growing pains as a divorced parent and as a single mother, and I have been turning back to *Letters to a Young Poet*, because I find very wise words, to me, not just as an artist, but even more so as a parent.

I believe that artists and books come into our lives when we are ready for them. When I read, I read with a preparedness to understand. I love to cruise bookstores and discover new artists. But when I go to the bookstore to choose books, I don't go with a dull sense just that I'm looking for something to read to pass the time. Instead, I go almost with the feeling that I'm looking for a bit of divine intervention—with a desire to be taught. Once I find authors I love, I tend to read all of their work.

About twenty years ago, I discovered Rilke. As I was reading his work *Sonnets to Orpheus*, I came across *Letters to a Young Poet*. I felt an immediate connection with this book and once I started to read it, I began clipping it to my script cover. I found myself referring back to it over and over again and learning something new each time.

Then I didn't read *Letters to a Young Poet* for a long time. In hindsight, I realize that the periods I haven't read it or referred back to it have been the darkest periods of my life. The refinding of this and several other books was a refinding of myself.

Books are like old friends to me and I think that reading is the greatest gift we can give to ourselves and others. I think that this is a book that helps people return to themselves and to return to their personal truths. I believe that, more than anything, we all want to find closeness with our core selves. I think we want to reconnect with a time when we used to run and play, drink out of a garden hose, and have a loyalty to ourselves and others. *Letters to a Young Poet* helps me to make that connection and it helps to refresh me into peacefulness.

February 23rd, 2009

RAAGESHWARI LOOMBA SWAROOP

"I experienced gratitude in a most powerful, miraculous way."

The Magic by Rhonda Byrne explains gratitude and its impact on the mind in a mystical, powerful way. I came upon this book five years back—close to the time it was released. I had been following Rhonda Byrne's work and I knew she was writing a new book, so I was very excited to read it.

I love that she explains gratitude in such a loving, childlike manner. I think she reaches so many different kinds of people and age groups because it is an easy, interactive book. It is on my bedside table and I refer to it on a daily basis.

It is not so much that this book transformed my beliefs, as that it reinforced them. Part of this is my belief in God. The more I read about science, the more I believe in God—as Einstein said. Science has proved that our thoughts and our words have a direct impact on our lives. Why do the poor keep getting poorer and the rich keep getting richer? Of course, there is poverty linked to horrific socioeconomic and geopolitical situations. However, many people are trapped in a cycle of poverty perpetuated by habitual negative thoughts. When they are young, many of these people learn that life is hard and that they have to work really, really hard to just get by. This becomes an affirmation, a self-fulfilling prophecy about the way life is.

However, I believe, and *The Magic* highlights, that whatever we focus on—whatever we believe—expands. In other words, we must be aware that when we think we are talking about problems in the present, we are actually signaling with our thoughts, our words, and our actions, that which will be manifested in our future. As Rhonda Byrne emphasizes, whatever you are grateful for becomes energy for your body. Anything that you are not grateful for becomes baggage. *The Magic* guides readers to focus on what they are grateful for. It is a one-month book that guides every adult, or child, on a different aspect of gratitude each day.

At age forty-one, I experienced gratitude in a most powerful, miraculous way—through the birth of my daughter, Samaya. Prior to her birth, I had actually had many health problems. I never talked about them. Quite the opposite—I focused on what I was grateful for. I treated my body as a temple; and although certain doctors and "experts" told me I could not have a child, I never had any doubt. I never experienced anxiety. Anxiety is like crimping a gardener's hose when she is trying to water the garden—the desire to water the garden can be there, but the plants do not get the nourishment they need.

Instead of feeling or focusing on anxiety or negative thoughts, each day, for many years, both before and after the birth of my daughter, I begin with my gratitude journal. I visualize my day in an idealized scenario and I write about it before anything in the day has actually happened. In this way, I feel gratitude for all the wonderful things that will happen before they actually occur. At the same time, I am aware of the importance of not becoming addicted to outcomes, because something may occur in my higher good that I had not anticipated.

Now I'm truly at a place where I rarely, very rarely judge people. My mind immediately starts affirming "to know all is to forgive all." The Dalai Lama pops in the windows of my mind, chanting that "love is the absence of judgment." There is actually no dearth in one's life but love. I have seen hearts melt, the stern faces smile, the rigid flow when introduced to love! And it only starts with gratitude!

Raageshwari

January 2nd, 2017

ROBERT TOWNE

"In this beautiful book, there are so many stories of heroic
lives lived, of matchless devotion, and enduring loyalty
and love."

Little Etsu-bo Sugimoto, author of *A Daughter of the Samurai*, was the youngest daughter of a much revered samurai warrior and grew up during the Restoration in 1870s Japan. Her home in the province of Echigo was virtually unchanged since the Middle Ages. So when Etsu-bo left her home in 1898 to come to America to marry a stranger and live in Cincinnati, she did more than travel across the world to an alien culture. She travelled through time, a thousand years into her future.

In recalling her home, she gave us a priceless look into a way of life that is heartbreaking to think is lost forever. The depth of feeling these people had for one another is almost impossible to convey. When little Etsu-bo was in her seventh-year celebration, she experienced a deep humiliation. All her women relatives were invited to a great feast and her hair had been elaborately arranged with Etsu-bo wearing a beautiful dress. At the celebration, Etsu-bo overheard one of her aunts saying, "It's a shameful waste to put a beautiful dress on Etsu-bo. It only attracts attention to her ugly, twisty hair." Etsu-bo was devastated and Ishi, her servant, overheard and saw Etsu-bo's reaction.

That night when Ishi came to undress her, Ishi had not removed the little blue-and-white towel that all Japanese servants wear over their hair when at work. Etsu-bo was surprised that her servant Ishi had appeared before a superior with her head covered for this was considered a mark of great disrespect. When Etsu-bo questioned her, she discovered the truth. Ishi had gone to the temple and cut off her splendid straight hair and placed it before the shrine, praying to the gods to transfer her hair to little Etsu-bo. As Etsu-bo wrote years later, "My good Ishi! My heart thanks her yet for her loving sacrifice."

Then there's the tale of Mr. Toda, a great samurai warrior like Etsu-bo's father. Like so many samurai, he had no understanding of money nor any way to make a living. Just a few short years before, Mr. Toda, sitting erect on his horse, would gallop by and all the young men would bow to him with their heads to the ground. Later, Mr. Toda, in a fancy hotel uniform, would bow these same fashionable young men into and out of the doors of the hotel as a way to make some sort of living. Brave and dignified Mr. Toda recognized that the new world wanted nothing to do with the culture of the old and accepted with calm dignity the fate of failure. But to Etsu-bo, he, like her father, remained a hero nevertheless.

In this beautiful book, there are so many stories of heroic lives lived, of matchless devotion, and enduring loyalty and love.

As Etsu-bo wrote, "Cherry blossoms never wither. They fall from the tree while still fresh and fragrant. Because of this the cherry blossom was chosen centuries ago as the symbol of the samurai spirit, willing to die while young and vigorous, rather than to live and fade."

Robt Towne

March 8th, 2017

LILY TUCK

"My life as a child was fairly solitary—hard to make friends if you cannot communicate—but it was not unhappy. I had books."

I was an only child and, on account of both the war (World War II) and my parents' divorce, I moved around a great deal—first from Paris, where I was born, to Lima, Peru, then to Montevideo, then back to Paris, and finally immigrating to New York in 1947 on a converted troop ship. My first language was French, then Spanish, then English. With each move, I was sent to a different school where I had to learn a new language, a new alphabet (the Spanish alphabet has twenty-nine letters—ch, ñ and ll—and although the French alphabet, like the English one, has only twenty-six letters, it has important accents and a cedilla). I also distinctly remember how when I finally arrived in America and was put in fourth grade—then there was no special education or remedial tutorials—the class was studying the Egyptians (there were drawings of pyramids and hieroglyphs pasted up on the classroom walls) and afraid I would be ridiculed, I never once, that whole year, opened my mouth. As a result, my life as a child was fairly solitary—hard to make friends if you cannot communicate—but it was not unhappy. I had books.

Also I was not lonely. For company, I made up stories—complicated stories about imaginary people, exciting events, and a beautiful piebald horse, named Tonto, which filled up my life. At the age of nine, I began writing a novel.

In *The Double Life of Liliane*, my latest novel, although a slightly fictionalized account of my life as a child and as an adolescent, I try to describe—dramatize is a better, more hopeful term—how the divided time I spent between my mother in New York and my father in Rome shaped me as a writer. In the last chapter of the novel, I also write about how a seminar I took on French symbolist poetry—Baudelaire, Rimbaud, and Mallarmé—my last year in college shaped me as a reader. The professor, Paul de Man, whose reputation, unfortunately, was later tarnished by an anti-Semitic article he wrote during the war in *Le Soir*, a Belgian newspaper, was one of the leading scholars who espoused deconstruction, the French popular literary theory of the time.

Deconstruction allows for the other to speak.

Deconstruction opens the text out to an affirmation of the absence of fixed meaning.

Deconstruction is opposed to binary thinking where one term is privileged over another i.e., Man/Woman, West/East.

Deconstruction involves placing oneself inside the text.

Etc.

Blond with Teutonic good looks and remarkably bright blue eyes, Paul de Man was mild mannered and soft-spoken. He began the seminar by quoting Blaise Pascal: "Quand on lit trop vite ou trop doucement on n'entend rien" (When one reads too quickly or too slowly, one hears nothing). He then went on to talk about allegory, a literary figure, where one thing refers to something else. A dove is the classic example. In a poem, the dove is a symbol of peace, but the reader also recognizes right away that the dove is a bird, even if, in the poem, it refers to something else. All narratives, de Man suggested, are allegories because of the gap between what the narrative does not say and what the reader does not say. A gap, in other words, between the reference and the referent. This may lead to misreading and misreading is an integral part of meaning, and, as a result, he said, meaning is always plural. For instance, in autobiographical texts—de Man mentioned Rousseau's *Confessions*, Wordsworth's *The Prelude*, and, of course, Proust's *À la recherche du temps perdu*—it is impossible to tell what is fact and what is fiction and impossible to tell whether figuration produces reference in a text or whether reference produces the figure. Instead, autobiography requires a form of substitution—exchanging the writing "I" for the written "I," and this implies that both persons are as different as they are the same. In the end, autobiography, de Man posited, is an act of self-restoration in which the author recovers the fragments of his or her life into a coherent narrative.

Paul de Man opened my mind and took me seriously. More specifically, he taught me how to read closely, how to intuitively interpret difficult texts, and how to view the authenticity of language.

Lily Tuck

September 15th, 2016

TED TURNER

"I felt that I was getting a double lesson: The history of ancient Greece and the history of our government in the United States."

Reading has been a very large and important part of my life. As a youngster, before the era of television, I listened to the radio in the afternoons and I learned history from historical movies. But most of all, I read.

This love of reading and history led me to Brown University, where I majored in classics and read many of the great works of ancient Greece. As a sophomore, I took a semester-long course with John Rowe Workman, who was the Mr. Chips of Brown and a famous author in his own right. He was the best professor I ever had and through his small class of about twenty students, I was introduced to *The History of the Peloponnesian War*, by Thucydides.

We spent an entire semester reading, dissecting, and discussing this book, which recounts the history of the war between Athens and Sparta in the fifth century BC. It also recounts the golden age of Athens, in the time of Pericles, who fostered the Athenian democracy—the first democracy in the world.

Before Professor Workman's class, I'd never spent so much time analyzing a book. It taught me a great deal about the ancient world. But, I was really inspired by the realization that, in reading *The History of the Peloponnesian War*, I was also learning about the origins of our government in the United States.

When our founding fathers—George Washington, Thomas Jefferson, Benjamin Franklin, and their peers—attended college, they studied history and language. But, they mostly studied the classics, including works by Virgil, Herodotus, and Thucydides. Later, they looked to works like *The History of the Peloponnesian War* and they drafted the Declaration of Independence and the Constitution, basically modeling them after the only successful democracy the world had ever known—that of Periclean Athens more than two thousand years before.

And so, in reading *The History of the Peloponnesian War*, I felt that I was getting a double lesson: the history of ancient Greece and the history of our government in the United States. The democratic experiment in Greece only lasted about fifty years until Athens was ultimately defeated by the combined forces of Greece, under the leadership of Sparta. However, through books such as *The History of the Peloponnesian War*, the Athenian democracy altered the fate of the world.

I think it is a shame that so few people read the classics. Great works such as *The History of the Peloponnesian War* have survived the test of time for more than two thousand years. They teach us about the ancient world and they help us to understand the evolution of history. Perhaps more importantly, truly great books, such as *The History of the Peloponnesian War*, also prompt us to examine the present. To this day, I think back to our analysis of *The History of the Peloponnesian War* in Professor Workman's class and draw parallels with current events, including the war with Iraq. It has helped me to understand the world in a different way, and it has been a true source of inspiration in my life.

December 1st, 2006

ARCHBISHOP DESMOND TUTU

"He let me consume comics omnivorously because he re-alized that it would help to instill a love of reading."

Looking back, I suppose there was always a fair amount of the escapist in me. Growing up in a three-roomed house in the squalor of Ventersdorp ghetto, I fed that escapist nature through books. I loved to read and be carried away on flights of fancy, into worlds in which the hero always ends up winning the race and riding into the sunset with the girl he has rescued from the machinations of the ungodly.

Even in the days before apartheid was imposed to refine and intensify racism, South Africa was defined by discrimination. My father was a schoolteacher and he clearly recognized that education was a tool that would help cut a path through that discrimination. As headmaster of his school, he stressed the importance of English, because he believed that English would give us access to great funds of knowledge that other languages wouldn't.

His conviction on this point was so strong that, except when we were learning Afrikaans or one of our vernaculars, he wouldn't let the schoolchildren use any other language than English. In fact, it was a punishable offense if we were caught speaking anything but English during school hours.

Then as now, there were people who said you mustn't let your children read comics because it isn't literature and it affects their language. My father, however, didn't agree. He let me consume comics omnivorously because he realized that it would help to instill a love of reading.

I still have fond memories of the Sub-Mariner, a hero from the lost island of Atlantis, who had the capacity to dive underwater and survive for long periods. Like the Greek god Mercury, the Sub-Mariner had wings on his feet, which enabled him to be fleet-footed in his quest to overcome the forces of evil. I was also very fond of the Lone Ranger, who went about on horseback sowing confusion among the ungodly.

Comic books eventually led me to more substantial books. When I was seven or eight, I discovered *Aesop's Fables* among the books on the shelf in our house. The anthology of fables transported me through marvelous fantasies that sparked my imagination. Later, when I was nine or ten, I found Lamb's *Tales from Shakespeare* on the same shelf. I was fascinated by the Shakespearean tales and that book genuinely sharpened my appetite for reading, which has remained a lifelong passion.

The comic books and the books that stand out from my youth spoke to me in many ways. Mostly, I think I was marked by them because they were saying that the universe is actually quite a moral universe, where evil and wrong do get their comeuppance and heroes can live happily ever after.

April 15th, 2005

"In fact, books have always played counterpoints to my pictures."

People often ask me, "How did you become a photographer?" I became a photographer in part because my father and my grandmother took pictures. But, I also became a photographer because I read a lot of books, which helped to foster a rich internal fantasy life.

This fantasy life started at an early age, but it was fueled by a wonderful English teacher I had in boarding school. He was the rebel teacher at school and we all loved his class. When we were supposed to be reading *The Scarlet Letter* by Hawthorne, he assigned *Another Country* by James Baldwin. But, he had us hide it within a copy of the assigned book in case the headmaster walked into class. I'll always remember him fondly because of that class, and because he turned me on to Willa Cather.

When I discover new authors. I tend to read all of their work. I was deeply moved by the words of Willa Cather and I continued to read her books throughout high school and college. I clearly remember when I arrived at *My Antonia*, because I fell in love with the book.

I was a student at Dennison University in Granville, Ohio, and it was a very cold winter. Late at night, while all my friends were off at fraternity parties drinking beer, I was snuggled in my bed with this amazing book. It is the story of Swedish immigrants crossing the country to settle in the plains around Red Cloud, Nebraska. I fell in love with this woman, Antonia, and I fell in love with the region of Nebraska through Cather's vivid descriptions.

Years later, one of my first assignments for British *Vogue* took me to Red Cloud for a photo shoot with the magazine's editor Elizabeth Tilberis. We went out to meet members of the Willa Cather Club, who showed us the house Cather lived in when she wrote *My Antonia* and the tree described in the book. These people were obsessed with Cather's writing. They knew every word she'd written and we had an incredible Willa Cather experience.

At the time, Liz was about to adopt her first child, and she was very nervous about it. We dressed all the children in town and put them in our fashion pictures with the models. Liz very much wanted to do a good job because it made her think about what it was going to be like to be a mom. It was an extraordinary moment of photography, fashion, and literature merging and becoming a great way to express myself in photographs.

Years later, Liz became editor of *Harper's Bazaar* in America and adopted her second child and we spoke fondly about our time in Red Cloud. Then, sadly, she was diagnosed with cancer and died. I was asked to speak at her memorial at Lincoln Center. I talked about the time we spent in Red Cloud, Nebraska, when none of us really planned anything and yet a lot of photos were taken of that small town and its people and put into the pages of British *Vogue*.

That shoot in Nebraska wasn't the only time elements of literature influenced my photographs. In fact, books have always played counterpoints to my pictures. The importance of literature in my life and in my work was once again apparent to me in compiling my new book, *Blood Sweat and Tears*, which includes photos from the Red Cloud shoot. This reminded me of my time in Nebraska with my dear friend Liz, the inspiration I'd derived from *My Antonia*, and the ways in which a book I'd read while snuggled in my bed as a college student on cold winter nights continued to touch my life in ways I never imagined.

Bruce Weber

April 12th, 2006

SIMON WIESENTHAL

"Each of us thought of the tragedies without number that this damp cellar bespoke, of the pious men and women from whom these holy books had been taken."

In Linz, shortly after the war, I heard that someone had found thousands of Jewish prayer books in the cellar of a sixteenth-century castle in Styria. Five of us drove to Styria to verify if this news were true. The castle lay in a remote forest; it was an unusually sinister-looking building, gray, dusty, and dilapidated. An old steward led us into the damp cellar and switched on a dim electric lamp. After our eyes grew accustomed to the poor lighting, we discovered enormous piles of black books, Bibles, prayer books, Talmud scrolls. Thousands and thousands lay there, like stacks of briquettes. The books came from the houses of Jews or synagogues from all over Europe. The rulers of the Third Reich had apparently intended to distribute the books to libraries, universities, and museums as historical curiosities, remnants of an extinct people that one day would be perhaps as valuable as Assyrian cuneiform tablets or statues from ancient Crete.

We stood there for a long time, unable to utter even a single word. Each of us thought of the tragedies without number that this damp cellar bespoke, of the pious men and women from whom these holy books had been taken.

The youngest member of our group was a young Jew from Carpatho-Ukraine, who had lost his entire family. Slowly he went past the piles of books, raised one or another up, brought it to his lips, and put it carefully back. Suddenly, behind me I heard a stifled scream. I turned around. There stood the young man with a prayer book in his hand. He stared at the first page, his face had become as pale as a corpse. He staggered then he collapsed. We ran to him. Our friend opened his eyes. His hands trembled. I picked the prayer book up off the ground and opened it. On the first page, I saw a handwritten entry, presumably from a woman. It must have been written in great agitation: "They just came into our city. In a few minutes they will be in our house. If someone should find this prayer book, I request that he notify my brother Benjamin XXX . . ."

Then there was a gap. Beneath it followed something, like a last minute postscript, written in great haste and almost illegible: "Don't forget us! And don't forget our murderers. They . . ." The handwriting broke off there.

I closed the book and looked at the young man. He was still white, but very calm. "If you don't mind, I would like to keep this book," he said. "It belonged to my sister. She died in Treblinka."

I have made the plea from that little prayer book my life's motto, to remind future generations—never to forget—will remain, until the end of my life, a mission I must fulfill.

February 24th, 2003

MUHAMMAD YUNUS

"We had a hunger to create our own world and books provided that world."

I was born in the village of Bathua, in Hathazari, Chittagong, which is the business center of Eastern Bengal, in what is now Bangladesh, in 1940. At the time, the entire subcontinent was part of the British Empire and we were in a turmoil of politics: British colonialism, the independence movement, and later, the creation of a new country.

Physically, we were in a very limited world. Of course, there was no internet and no television, but there were also no telephones and just one radio that broadcast mostly government programs that were not very good. Compare that to the connectivity of today. The *Encyclopedia Britannica* would have been the ultimate treasure for us when I was a child. Today, many children have never heard of the *Encyclopedia Britannica* and they don't need it, because they have the internet. There are multiple people chatting away with each other simultaneously on any number of topics in chat rooms and even young children have cell phones.

Of course, we couldn't have imagined any of this in my village in Bangladesh in the 1940s and 1950s. Books were the only way we could connect with the rest of the world and, through reading, I became ever more curious about other people and other countries.

We lived in a two-room house with a large family. Consequently, we grew up in the back of shops and in the streets and it was hard for us to imagine the people and places described in books. But, we had a hunger to create our own world and books provided that world—they took us beyond what we could physically see and experience.

However, we had limited access to books, because our school didn't have a library until we reached high school: This scarcity of books led me to my first important project, which was building a personal library of the books I collected from around the age of nine or ten. I had seven brothers—two of us, my older brother and I, eventually accumulated a library of two hundred books, written in Bengali, in different genres, including fiction, nonfiction, and poetry.

This was not easy, because we had very little money. We only received a small amount of money to eat snacks at school. I didn't eat snacks, I didn't go to the movies, and I didn't do many other things so that I could buy books. Later, I won a scholarship in my class—a small amount of money—it too went to buying books.

That library was so important to me. But, at the time, I didn't think it was something unusual—it was just something that was good and something that seemed right. We had a little shelf and we wanted to fill it up with books. This desire came from our curiosity—we wanted to read the books that would fill that shelf.

It was a very serious process. My brother and I stamped, numbered, and cataloged all the books. We recorded where the book came from and how we got the copy. These books opened my world and the library eventually became a lending library for local children—we even had an exchange program. Thus, the little project that started on a shelf in our small house enriched the lives of many.

Unfortunately, millions of people the world over do not have access to the books that would enrich their lives. If you are not reading books, or if you cannot read books because you have no access to them or because you are illiterate, you are like a blind person or someone whose eyesight works for only one meter. You see only a tiny little thing in front of you or a tiny little area around you, when the world is so big, and diverse, and wonderful.

It is true today that there are many substitutes for books. But, I would say that books still have their own place—they are not something to be relegated to a museum. We need writers who formulate words and sentences in powerful ways and in powerful books that teach us, inspire us, spark our imaginations, and stick in our minds.

Whether people choose to read books of fiction or history, books of poetry or, like me as a young boy, biographies of great leaders and despots, their hearts and their minds will open to the tremendous potential in the world, and the tremendous potential within themselves.

February 18th, 2009

AFTERWORD BY LIAM NEESON

As you turn to this page, you reach the end of a unique journey through the stories of how reading and books have touched the lives of people whose lives have touched the world.

I cannot help but reflect on how this journey began for me more than twenty years ago, when I was filming *Before and After* in the Berkshires of western Massachusetts. The crew was quite small, especially in the beginning, and that is how I came to know James Owens, the editor of this volume, who was working as a production assistant.

I noticed that whenever he was on break he seemed to be reading books. Since I am also a voracious reader, I inevitably asked him about what he was reading. This was the start of a friendship—a friendship that grew from books and reading.

Later during the production, I learned from my assistant Kelly that James would be working on his thirtieth birthday. By that time I had learned about his Irish roots, and I remember giving him a book as his birthday present, *A Day in the Life of Ireland*.

At that time Natasha was expecting our first child Micheál, and James also came to know her when she visited the set. It seems a very long time ago, but they are happy memories.

James and I remained friends. In 2002 when he asked me to be part of a book he conceived called *The World is Just a Book Away*, I immediately said "yes," because books have played such an important role in my life and my career. I also immediately knew that I wanted to write about *David Copperfield* by Charles Dickens, because it is the book that sparked my love of reading and understanding of characters in ways that moved me and that helped me connect more deeply with the characters I portray as an actor. Natasha was just as excited about the idea and a bit later her mother, Vanessa Redgrave, also joined the project.

At the same time, none of us imagined it would take James fifteen years to complete the book. Yet, I am struck by how the journey of creating the book in many ways mirrors the journey of life. We start out on a path, but we encounter twists and turns, valleys and hills, and we end up some place completely different from where we expected to be.

It is a great privilege to be exposed to something in its infancy—when it is just a kernel of an idea—and to watch it grow. It is like watching a child grow through the phases of life.

That has been my experience with *The World is Just a Book Away*, from when James first told me about the book, to when he told me about his idea to start a literacy charity with the same name (WIJABA for short), which has now served tens of thousands of underprivileged children in three countries.

The World is Just a Book Away is very personal to me, of course, because it relates—through my submission as well as those of Natasha and Vanessa—the importance of reading through five generations of our family (from a book belonging to Vanessa's great-aunt to books we read to our sons). Natasha and I were reading children's stories to our boys when we wrote our submissions, and they are grown young men today. It gives me great pleasure to know that part of the legacy we shared with them is their love of reading.

At the same time I recognize that *The World is Just a Book Away* is much more than just a book to which I feel a personal connection. I do not believe that reading the afterword will be the final step on a reader's journey with this book. *The World is Just a Book Away* is not a book to be read once and given away or stuck in the back of a closet. This is a book that should be kept on a nightstand or placed on a special shelf and visited time and again, like an old friend. Whenever we need inspiration for what to read next—for our own pleasure or to our children and grandchildren—we can turn to *The World is Just a Book Away*.

August 30th, 2017

ABOUT THE WORLD IS JUST A BOOK AWAY (WIJABA)

The World is Just a Book Away (WIJABA) is an international children's literacy charity founded in 2008 to inspire hope through education. Based on a love of books, reading, and learning, WIJABA is helping to combat the cycle of illiteracy and poverty in order to encourage peace around the world.

We believe that we can change lives book by book, library by library, and child by child. Our mission is to promote literacy and education by developing libraries and programs that plant the seeds of leadership, environmental consciousness, and community connection.

It is a belief that we have put into practice by reaching more than seventy thousand children in Indonesia, Mexico, and the United States through ninety libraries, two mobile libraries, and the WIJABA Environmental Education Program in Partnership with Jane Goodall's Roots & Shoots.

Through the generous support of our donors, we provide children with access to books and educational programs that are essential to literacy. We know that learning follows books, and that hope follows learning into the communities we serve.

To learn more about how you can help children have access to books, quality education, and hope for the future, please visit www.wijaba.org.

ABOUT THE ILLUSTRATOR

Ryane Acalin is an artist who works in mixed media, pencil, and ink to produce portraiture and large-scale scenes that focus on the temporal spectrum of human existence. Her work has been exhibited at galleries, universities, and in private and corporate collections. She is the artist and cocreator of the graphic novel *Cinder's Kingdom*. She studied at UC Berkeley and lives in Venice, California.

For more information please visit www.ryaneacalin.com.

ABOUT THE EDITOR

James J. Owens is a professor of management communication at the University of Southern California Marshall School of Business. He is founder and CEO of the charity The World is Just a Book Away (WIJABA), which promotes children's literacy internationally by developing libraries and educational programs. Since its inception in 2008, WIJABA has touched the lives of more than seventy thousand children. James collected and edited the sixty essays in this book over the course of fifteen years. His profit from this book will benefit the charity. James is also a writer and a speaker. He lives with his son Alexander in Santa Monica, California.

To learn more, please visit www.wijaba.org.